Books should be returned or renewed by the last
date above. Renew by phone **03000 41 31 31** or
online *www.kent.gov.uk/libs*   21 DEC 2023

_____

_____

Libraries Registration & Archives

CUSTOMER SERVICE EXCELLENCE

Kent
County
Council
kent.gov.uk

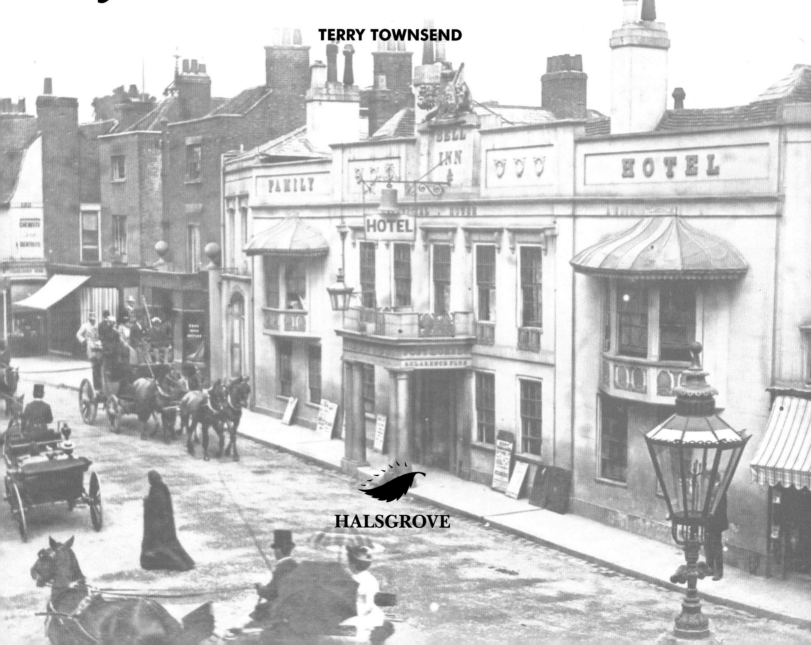

• HALSGROVE DISCOVER SERIES ➤

Jane Austen's Kent

TERRY TOWNSEND

HALSGROVE

For Carol
who has encouraged and helped me with every aspect of this book.

'Kent is the only place for happiness'
Jane Austen, 8 December 1798

First published in Great Britain in 2015

Copyright © Terry Townsend 2015

British Library Cataloguing-in-Publication Data
A CIP record for this title is available from the British Library

ISBN 978 0 85704 257 6

HALSGROVE
Halsgrove House, Ryelands Business Park,
Bagley Road, Wellington, Somerset TA21 9PZ
Tel: 01823 653777   Fax: 01823 216796
email: sales@halsgrove.com

Part of the Halsgrove group of companies.
Information on all Halsgrove titles is
available at: www.halsgrove.com

Printed in China by the Everbest Printing Co Ltd

Contents

Acknowledgements

I would particularly like to thank
Adrienne Bradney-Smith for generously sharing her knowledge
and advising on the manuscript as a whole.
Brenda Stables for her encouragement and editorial help.
I would also like to admit the debt I owe
to the scholarship of Deirdre Le Faye.

A big thank you goes to the following people who
allowed me access to their homes, estates and businesses.

Jason Hollands, Broadford, Horsmonden.
Phyllis Tanzer, Grovehurst, Horsmonden.
Knocker & Foskett Solicitors, The Red House, Sevenoaks.
Mrs Jan Gray, The Grey House, Seal.
Eliza Ecclestone, St Clere, Kemsing.
Princess Olga Romanoff, Provender near Ospringe.
Margaret, Lady FitzWalter, Goodnestone.
Mrs Fiona Sunley, Godmersham Park.
Miss Rebecca Lilley BA Hons, Godmersham Park Heritage Centre.
Tessa Wheeler, Chilham Castle.
Nick Sandford MRICS, Godinton House Preservation Trust.
Mr T. F. Parrett and Isobel Howard of Eastwell Manor Hotel.
The staff of Broome Park, Barham.
Jane Hardy, Sandling Park.
Mrs Jane Clark, Saltwood Castle.
Plus
Barbara Byne, St Laurence church, Ramsgate.
Terry Wheeler of the Ramsgate Historical Society.

Map of the places featured in this book

10. Goodnestone
11. Godmersham
12. Chilham
13. Canterbury
14. Ashford & Godinton
15. Eastwell

1. Horsmonden
2. Tonbridge
3. Sevenoaks
4. Seal & Kemsing
5. Bromley

6. Westerham
7. Dartford
8. Rochester
9. Ospringe, Norton
   & Provender

16. Lenham
17. Barham
18. Ramsgate
19. Deal
20. Sandling & Saltwood
21. Wrotham

Introduction

This watercolour of Jane was painted by her sister Cassandra around 1810 by which time both sisters had acquired an intimate knowledge of Kent, the county of their forebears.

J ane Austen had knowledge and experience of most of England's southern counties but the two she knew intimately were Hampshire and Kent.

Much has been written about Jane's connection with the Hampshire villages of Steventon and Chawton. She was born at Steventon in her father's rectory and spent the majority of her first twenty-five years in this area of gentle, rolling countryside. Her home and the Steventon neighbourhood became the cradle for her talent and are reflected in her novels. Towards the end of her sadly short life the cottage at Chawton, which now welcomes visitors from around the world, provided the secure environment for her literary genius to flourish.

Much less has been written about the major part of her life's experience gained in Kent. Prolonged holidays in the county afforded much happiness as well as inspiration and material for her books. Jane's family were from Kent and many of her relatives lived in the county. She visited them while still a young girl and it was later here in Kent she gained detailed knowledge of the country-house life of her time.

Jane's paternal ancestry can be traced back through seven generations of yeoman farmers who had established themselves in the Weald of Kent over a period of two-and-a-half centuries. Jane's father, the Reverend George Austen was born in Tonbridge and spent his formative years in this ancient town on the River Medway. The Hampshire clerical livings he later received were in the gift of Kentish relations.

Jane's father, the Reverend George Austen, was born in Tonbridge and spent his formative years in the ancient town on the River Medway.

Growing up in the Steventon Rectory Jane and her siblings would have heard many family stories of Kent even before they visited the county themselves. When Jane was eight, further Kentish connections were established when Rev'd George Lefroy brought his beautiful wife Anne and their children to live in the rectory at Ashe, an adjoining parish two miles to the north.

The Lefroys were the Austen's nearest neighbours and despite the age discrepancy, a special friendship developed between Anne 'a perfect model of gracefulness and

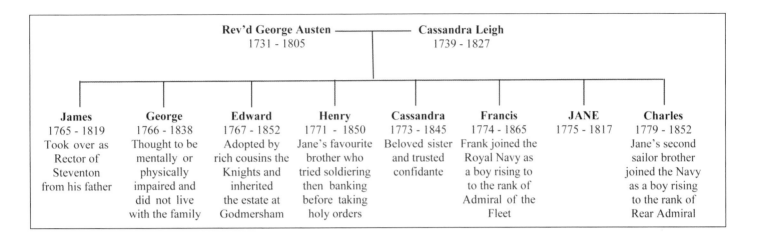

Rev'd George Austen 1731 - 1805			Cassandra Leigh 1739 - 1827				
James 1765 - 1819 Took over as Rector of Steventon from his father	**George** 1766 - 1838 Thought to be mentally or physically impaired and did not live with the family	**Edward** 1767 - 1852 Adopted by rich cousins the Knights and inherited the estate at Godmersham	**Henry** 1771 - 1850 Jane's favourite brother who tried soldiering then banking before taking holy orders	**Cassandra** 1773 - 1845 Beloved sister and trusted confidante	**Francis** 1774 - 1865 Frank joined the Royal Navy as a boy rising to to the rank of Admiral of the Fleet	**JANE** 1775 - 1817	**Charles** 1779 - 1852 Jane's second sailor brother joined the Navy as a boy rising to the rank of Rear Admiral

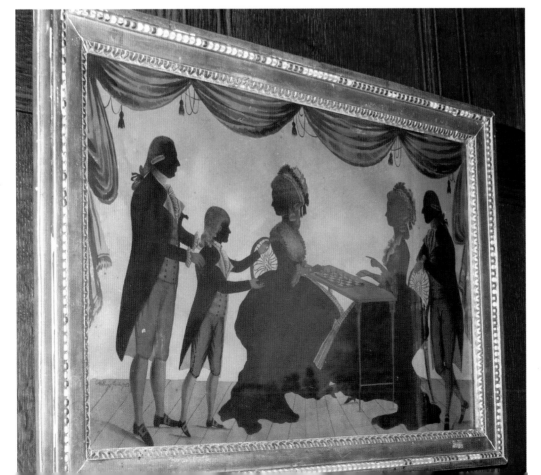

This illustration, which hangs in Chawton House Library, depicts the moment when Jane's twelve-year-old brother Edward was officially presented to Thomas and Catherine Knight of Godmersham Park in Kent who became his adoptive parents.

Anne Lefroy 'a perfect model of gracefulness and goodness' moved to the Steventon neighbourhood from Wootton Court in Kent and became a mentor and special friend to Jane.

goodness' and the younger Jane who became a frequent visitor to the Lefroy home. Anne was the eldest of eight children born to Edward and Jemima Brydges of Wootton Court, located between Canterbury and Dover. It would not be too fanciful to think Anne would have told Jane about her own adolescent years, of the romance of balls and parties held at the great houses during an age of unsurpassed elegance.

Our first knowledge of Jane being in Kent is on 22 July 1788. She was twelve-and-a-half and had arrived in Sevenoaks with her parents and sister Cassandra to stay for a month at The Red House, home to ninety-year-old Great Uncle Francis Austen. By this time the Rev'd George Austen had become well established in Steventon with his wife Cassandra Leigh and their eight children: James, George, Edward, Henry, Cassandra, Frank, Jane and Charles. As his offspring approached their teenage years it was George Austen's habit to take them on an extended trip to West Kent, primarily to present them to Uncle Francis who had been his benefactor.

The Austen's third son Edward was born in 1767 and was later adopted by distant Kentish cousins. This event was ultimately to provide Jane with great opportunities to explore the county and its social life.

Cassandra, Jane's beloved sister, was born in 1773 and the following year saw the birth of Francis (Frank), the first of Jane's two sailor brothers. When stationed in Kent, Frank met and married a Kentish girl, Mary Gibson from Ramsgate. This further extended Jane's opportunity for travel and she visited the Kent coast at the time it was under threat of invasion by Napoleon's armies.

As well as being a guide to the Kentish places significant in the Austen family history, this book is also an exploration of the locations Jane knew personally. The journey takes us to pretty villages, pleasant market towns and the historic cities of Canterbury and Rochester. We visit great estates where Jane was a frequent and welcome guest; churches where she worshipped; venues where she danced and the turnpike roads along which she travelled recounting varying experiences at coaching inns.

Most of our information concerning Jane's experience of Kent comes from the letters she wrote to Cassandra on occasions when the sisters were apart. There are also references to her being present in Kent in other people's letters and journals, plus biographical reminiscences from her nieces and nephews.

Unfortunately for us, Cassandra chose to censor and destroy the majority of Jane's letters after her sister's death which leaves tantalising gaps in our information. There are some places in Kent which seem obvious Jane would have visited but documented proof is wanting. What we have is rather like a large jig-saw puzzle with pieces missing. We have a very good overall picture and even a reasonable idea of the shape and pattern of the missing pieces but, on occasion, probability has to play a part.

We begin our journey at Horsmonden in the richly cultivated countryside of the Kentish Weald where Austens lived for centuries before Jane was born.

Francis, the first of Jane's two sailor brothers, married a Kentish girl, Mary Gibson from Ramsgate.

Above: *Cassandra Austen 1773-1845. Most of our information concerning Jane's experience of Kent comes from the letters she wrote to her beloved sister who was two years her senior.*

Left: *Jane Austen 1775 - 1817.*

1. Horsmonden

The Austen family roots are firmly planted in the clay of the Kentish Weald. The family became established in what is now the richly cultivated countryside in the south west of the county. This area, lying between the parallel chalk escarpments of the North and the South Downs, was once the thickly wooded forest of 'Andredsweald' where the early Austens would have been involved in iron making, a process which used ironstone from various clay beds and was fuelled by charcoal made from the trees.

In addition to charcoal making, the timber was used for construction and ship-building. Henry VIII's warships were made from Wealden Oak. As the forest was cleared the iron industry declined in this part of England and the manufacturing process moved north to be fuelled by coke made from coal.

The main employment in the area gradually inclined towards sheep farming and the Austens became involved in the cloth trade, with spinning and weaving as a cottage industry in villages. Initial modest fortunes were enlarged by succeeding generations of Austens who flourished and earned their place among the wealthiest wool merchants in the county. Their names were proudly enrolled alongside the Bathursts and Courthorpes in the annals of the prosperous company of woollen traders known as 'the Grey Coats of Kent'. They became power-brokers at county elections and owners of substantial manor house properties.

Our journey begins at the Wealden village of Horsmonden where Tudor homesteads and timbered cottages gather round a spacious village green. Looking around the scene, it becomes apparent there is something missing – there is no church. This village, like others in England, relocated a mile or so away from its original centre in the mid fourteenth century to escape the pestilence of the Black Death.

For 600 years St Margaret's church, with its Austen family memorials, has stood in open farmland. The isolated position can be appreciated from the hill on which the village of Goudhurst stands. This view of the church with its neighbouring farms and cluster of hop-drying oasthouses, would be little different from Kentish rural scenes familiar to Jane.

The Austen family name was originally spelt Astyn and Jane's paternal line can be traced with reasonable certainty back to William Astyn who died in 1522. By 1574 William's son Stephen had been granted official permission to bear the coat of arms of the

St Margaret's church Horsmonden, with its Austen family memorials, has stood for the past 600 years in open Wealden farmland with only a few agricultural buildings for neighbours.

This ornate gated table-top tomb is not far from the south wall of the church. It marks the grave of John Austen VI who died in 1807, his wife Joan and his daughter Mary. The Austen monogram is incorporated in the railings.

11

Preserved under a carpet in the nave of
St Margaret's is this memorial tablet to the
Austens of Horsmonden with the family's
coat of arms at the top.

*The memorial brass for Joan Berry,
wife of John Austen I (1560-1620),
is also protected by the carpet.*

Astyn family at Yalding. This heraldic sanction was extended to the branch of the Astyns who came from Chevening near Sevenoaks.

Robert Astyn, Stephen's eldest son by his second wife, was the father of the first John Austen of Horsmonden who was born in 1560 during the reign of Elizabeth I. From here, Jane's ancestry can be traced directly through seven generations of Kentish yeomen all named John Austen. In the floor of the nave of St Margaret's a large memorial tablet to Austen family members displays a worn shield bearing the Austen coat of arms.

Close to this family grave is a brass memorial to Joan Berry who is shown dressed in a splendid Jacobean costume. Joan was the wife of John Austen I who, after bearing him seven children, died giving birth to twins. Perhaps Joan was able to take solace from her deep personal Christian faith; the wording on her memorial reads: 'let neither hvsband nor children nor lands nor goods separate me from my god'.

The Austen family consolidated their wool business with the purchase of land and property. A large number of houses in the village appear to have been built or owned by members of the Austen family. These include the impressive Tudor manor houses of Grovehurst and Broadford. Joan and John's fifth son, Francis Austen I of Horsmonden (1600–1687) was Jane's great-great-great-grandfather and it is probable that Francis acquired Broadford and Grovehurst. Francis's son John Austen III, Jane's great-great-

Grovehurst dating to the early 1600s was the home of the earlier members of the Austen family, many of whose graves can be seen in the churchyard of St Margaret's in Horsmonden.

Grovehurst was originally a Wealden Hall House where smoke from an open central fire would have escaped through an opening in the roof.

Broadford, another Wealden Hall House was the home of Jane Austen's great-grandfather, the fourth John Austen. He died of consumption in 1704 leaving his wife Elizabeth with considerable debts and seven children under ten.

grandfather, was born at Grovehurst in 1629 and died there in 1705.

As we move into the early eighteenth century, things become more specific to Jane Austen and we see how resultant events were to impact on her life. The eldest son of John Austen III, also named John, married Jane Atkins and had two sons and three daughters. The marriages of the three daughters are recorded on the same family memorial tablet in the nave of St Margaret's which bears the Austen family arms.

One of the daughters called Jane (by now an established family name), married Stephen Stringer of Goudhurst and their granddaughter (also named Jane) married Thomas Brodnax of Godmersham, near Canterbury – an event with particular significance for the Austens.

With Thomas we come across the curious practice of name changing in anticipation of inheritance, which is a recurring theme in Jane's family story. Thomas Brodnax had been born Thomas May but changed his name to Brodnax in order to inherit an estate. Changing one's name, however, required an Act of Parliament.

When a distant cousin bequeathed him her Hampshire estates at Steventon and

From 1574 The Astyn and later the Austen families were permitted to display a coat of arms. Unfortunately the Austen crest which was once part of this carving in the entrance hall of Broadford no longer exists.

Chawton, Thomas found it worthwhile to change his name once more, this time to Knight. His rapid changes of name provoked one Member of Parliament to comment: 'This gentleman gives us so much trouble that the best way would be to pass an Act for him to use whatever name he pleases.'

Thomas's son, Thomas Knight II, became a great benefactor to Jane Austen's family and the catalyst for her experience of East Kent. Thomas and his wife Catherine Knatchbull had no children of their own and by mutual agreement adopted Jane's brother Edward. Edward remained an Austen until after his adopted father's death when Mrs Knight passed the Steventon and Chawton estates on to him, together with the Kent property of Godmersham.

These weavers' cottages, seen from the churchyard of Goudhurst, are typical of the medieval homes workplaces where the spinning and weaving took place.

Finally we come to Jane's great grandfather John IV, who resided at Broadford in Horsmonden and inherited the flourishing wool business and additional property. In 1693 he married Elizabeth Weller of Tonbridge who, at that stage, must have been confident of a secure future. Unfortunately, unforeseeable events and flaws in her husband's character denied her promised opportunities. John died of consumption in 1704, the year before his own father, leaving Elizabeth with seven children under ten to raise and considerable unforeseen debts.

The next part of the story reveals how Elizabeth dealt with this dilemma to emerge as the heroine of the Austen saga.

2. Tonbridge

Before moving to Broadford on her marriage to John Austen IV, Elizabeth Weller had been brought up in a substantial property in Bordyke called Chauntlers. Her grandfather, Thomas Weller, who had acquired the house in 1631, was a Parliamentarian who played an important role in the English Civil War. His own accounts of what took place in and around Tonbridge and inside Chauntlers itself make exciting reading and perhaps suggest the source of Elizabeth's inherited resourcefulness and determination.

With the untimely death of her husband, Jane's great-grandmother faced a dilemma. How was she to pay off his debts and raise a large family as a single parent? At first she turned for help to her father-in-law, John Austen III of Grovehurst. He was very wealthy but, as she wrote: 'loath to part with anything'. Although previously promising his dying son that 'he would not have him troubled by his debts' and he would consider his son's children equally, it transpired he was interested only in helping the son and heir, John Austen V.

The old man said the funeral should be as private as possible and even refused to provide expenses of £10 to buy mourning clothes for the widow and children. After much argument he eventually agreed to part with £200 towards his son's debts but on the day before the money was to be paid he died.

It seems probable that John V attended Tonbridge School before going up to Pembroke College, Cambridge. Later, inheriting the family home at Broadford, he married his cousin Mary Stringer by whom he had three children; John VI, Jane (previously mentioned) and Elizabeth. After an unremarkable and short life he died at the age of thirty-two and is buried at Horsmonden.

Elizabeth is the first Austen whose writing survives today and a copy of her 'Memorandum' is on display in Tonbridge church. This unique document gives an account of her widowhood and her strategy for coping with the crisis: 'it seemed to me, as if I could not do a better thing for my Children's good, their education being my great care… for I always tho't if they had learning they might ye better shift in ye world.'

In *Persuasion* Jane echoes this sentiment, adding also that boys fared better than girls when it came to education: 'men have had every advantage of us in telling their own story. Education has been theirs in so much higher a degree' said Anne Elliot to Captain Harville.

Chauntlers in Bordyke, where Jane's great-grandmother was brought up is now divided into two: The Priory and The Red House.

Faced with coping single-handedly with the future of her daughter and the five remaining sons (Jane's great uncles) Elizabeth sold some possessions to help pay off the debts then rented out Broadford before taking the job of housekeeper for Elijah Fenton, the headmaster at Sevenoaks School.

Part of the agreement was that her boys would receive an education at reduced fees. Tonbridge School might seem the more obvious choice but the headmaster there at the time had a wife to undertake the domestic requirements. He also had a poor reputation as an educationalist, particularly compared with the brilliant Fenton.

By studying the progress of Elizabeth's sons, we can begin to recognise events that were to impact on Jane's life.

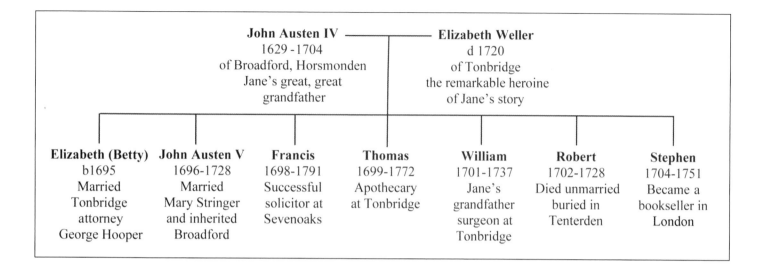

John Austen IV ———————— **Elizabeth Weller**
1629 - 1704   d 1720
of Broadford, Horsmonden   of Tonbridge
Jane's great, great   the remarkable heroine
grandfather   of Jane's story

Elizabeth (Betty)	**John Austen V**	**Francis**	**Thomas**	**William**	**Robert**	**Stephen**
b1695	1696-1728	1698-1791	1699-1772	1701-1737	1702-1728	1704-1751
Married	Married	Successful	Apothecary	Jane's	Died unmarried	Became a
Tonbridge	Mary Stringer	solicitor at	at Tonbridge	grandfather	buried in	bookseller in
attorney	and inherited	Sevenoaks		surgeon at	Tenterden	London
George Hooper	Broadford			Tonbridge		

Elizabeth's second son Francis (1698-1791), known to Jane and her family as Old Mr Francis Austen of Sevenoaks, became the most successful of the brothers and his career and the influence he had on Jane's life are covered in the following chapter.

In 1715, Elizabeth's third son, Thomas was apprenticed to Henry Wells, a London haberdasher for a premium of £160. He later became an apothecary and returned to Tonbridge to practice. Thomas married Elizabeth Burgess and they lived in the now beautifully restored medieval Blair House at 186 High Street.

Their son Henry, whom the Austens called Harry, was George's cousin and therefore Jane's first cousin once removed. He attended Tonbridge School before becoming a fellow of Clare College, Cambridge in 1748. Following his graduation and ordination he was presented with the Perpetual Curacy of St Giles' church at Shipbourne, 3 miles north of the town.

At Michaelmas, two years later, Elizabeth's only daughter Betty (born 1695), ceased to be a financial burden: 'Now Betty is of Age to receive what her Grandfather Left her I don't reckon any thing here on her account this qr.' Shortly after this Betty became completely independent when she married George Hooper, a well-to-do Tonbridge attorney.

Elizabeth's fourth son William (1701-1737), who was to become Jane's paternal grandfather, was just three years old when his father died. After completing his Sevenoaks schooling in 1717, William was apprenticed to Woolwich surgeon William Ellis, for a fee of £115.10s.

It is interesting to note that in Jane's time apothecaries and surgeons were not counted among other professions or the gentry. When giving advice to her aspiring novelist niece Anna Lefroy, in a letter of 10 August 1814, Jane says: 'a Country Surgeon would not be introduced to Men of their rank'. Like his elder brother Thomas, William also returned to Tonbridge to practice.

Robert, the unmarried fifth son died of smallpox aged twenty-six and is buried in Tenterden. Stephen, the sixth and youngest, became a bookseller in the area of St Paul's Churchyard, London. He chose to remain in London following his apprenticeship to stationer William Innys in 1719.

Jane's grandfather William Austen lived at 174 High Street, Tonbridge. The building was later used as a furniture retailing business but was tragically destroyed by fire in

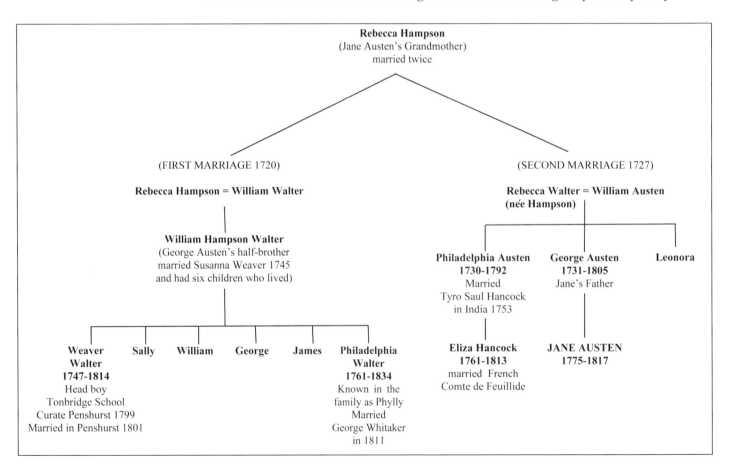

1997. A new block of shops and offices now occupies the site.

In 1727 William married his first wife Rebecca, the daughter of Gloucester physician Sir George Hampson. Rebecca, was the widow of William Walter and already had a son William Hampson Walter from her first marriage.

William Austen had four children with Rebecca. Their first, a daughter called Hampson died at two years of age. Another daughter Philadelphia, Jane's aunt, followed in 1730. Next was Jane's father George, born in 1731, followed by a third daughter Leonora the following year. From this rather complicated family tree we can see that William Hampson Walter was half-brother to George Austen and, though he was ten years older than George, the two kept contact throughout their lives.

Rebecca died in 1732 shortly after Leonora's birth and for four years William Austen's children were motherless. In 1736 William married for a second time and his new wife, Susanna Kelk, was thirteen years his senior. She accepted the three step-children, Philadelphia, George and Leonora, until William died a year later in 1737 when she sent them to live with her husband's relatives.

At first George lived with his uncle, Stephen, but it was an unsuccessful arrangement and he returned to Tonbridge to live with aunt Betty in her house in East Street, then called Powells but now known as Lyons.

Lyons in East Street, previously known as Powells where Jane's father George came to live after his father's death.

Tonbridge School

A plaque on the wall of the Cawthorn Lecture Theatre, situated at the front of Tonbridge School, informs us that: 'The Reverend George Austen M.A., father of Jane Austen, was a pupil here 1741-1747 and Second Master 1754-1757'. It was George's Uncle Francis from Sevenoaks who arranged the schooling and paid the fees.

Tonbridge School where Jane's father was enrolled aged ten.

The plaque displayed on the wall of the Cawthorn Lecture Theatre, Tonbridge School.

Arriving at the school as a ten-year-old orphan it must have been a comfort to George to know his cousin Harry was already established as head boy.

George received an excellent education, winning a school scholarship and bursary which enabled him to go to Oxford. After university and his ordination he returned to Tonbridge to teach. The headmaster, James Cawthorn chose George for the position of Second Master and among the pupils at the school was Francis Motley Austen, Uncle Francis's son. During this period George took over the curacy of Shipbourne from his cousin Harry.

Tonbridge Castle

Tonbridge Castle was built at the time of the Norman Conquest. After the Civil War it was sold into private hands and Thomas Weller, Jane's great-great-great-grandfather, acquired the lease. By 1739 the castle was owned by John Hooker and it passed to his son Thomas.

This house of medieval origin was home to Thomas Austen, apothecary and his wife Elizabeth Burgess. In later years it was known as The Star and The White Horse Inn.

Tonbridge Castle is one of England's finest examples of a motte and bailey. The Georgian house to the right of the splendid thirteenth-century gatehouse was built in 1791 by John Hooker using stones from the ruined walls of the castle.

Jane's favourite brother Henry was taken to meet the Kentish relations in 1780 and 1783. In his old age he recorded memories of the trips.

Among Jane Austen's relatives buried in a grave in the north aisle is her grandfather William. The gravestone is covered for preservation but this photograph showing part of the inscription can be seen on the north wall.

In 1763 Harry Austen married Thomas's sister Mary Hooker, so the castle entered the Austen family story.

The handsome Georgian mansion which stands today next to the gatehouse was built in 1791 by John Hooker using stones from the ruined walls of the castle. Stone from the towers, walls and keep had been used earlier in 1741 in the construction of the Medway Canal.

In 1898 the castle was sold to Tonbridge Urban District Council and nearly a century later the gatehouse was opened to the public. Today audio tours are available which tell the story of the castle's 900 year long history which, in addition to the Austens, is interwoven with that of kings and archbishops, tyrants and heroes, murderers and mercenaries.

Tonbridge Parish Church

Parts of Tonbridge's parish church are as old as the castle. Generations of Austens have worshipped and are remembered here. Jane's grandfather, William is buried here with Rebecca, his first wife, and two year-old Hampson. William's second wife Susanna, who outlived him, is also buried here. The gravestone is covered by a carpet for preservation but there is a photograph of the inscription on the adjacent wall.

Jane's father, his half-brother and his sisters were all christened here. Copies of the relevant entries from the parish register are on display in a case inside the entrance to the church, along with other fascinating Austen memorabilia.

In a way, the connection with Tonbridge church comes full circle in Jane's story. A list of incumbents includes the name of Rev'd John Rawston Papillon who was vicar here from 1791 until 1802 when he became Rector at Chawton, the Hampshire village where six years later Jane Austen, her mother and sister came to live. It became an Austen family joke, which Jane took in good part, that one day she would marry the nervous and twitchy rector who was twelve years her senior. Both John Papillon and his sister Elizabeth appear frequently in Jane's surviving letters.

Another name on the list of incumbents is that of the Rev'd Henry Harpur, uncle of J.M.W. Turner, who stayed with him in Tonbridge to paint local scenes. Harpur oversaw Jane's father during his first curacy at Shipbourne.

In 1780 Rev'd George Austen and his wife travelled from Hampshire to introduce their nine-year-old son Henry to the Kentish relations. In his old age, Henry recorded memories of the trip, describing his meeting with Great Uncle Francis. In 1783 Henry again visited Kent with his parents and this time his young brother Frank was included in the party. Tonbridge is only 7 miles from Sevenoaks so it seems likely George would have taken his children to see where he was born and went to school.

It is also natural he would have taken them to meet his cousin Harry, his wife Mary Hooker and their three children who lived in a property at 182 High Street called Fosse

There are a number of family memorials in the church of St Peter and St Paul where the Austen family worshipped.

Bank (named after the town's early defences), which his brother-in-law Thomas Hooker had vacated. They later downsized into the house next door, number 180, which until recently, was the offices of Warner's Solicitors. Frank recalled visiting Tonbridge when cousin Harry's son, nine-year-old Edgar, played a practical joke on him which involved being stabbed by a pin.

In the next chapter we will see Jane in her thirteenth year spending a month in West Kent with her parents and sister visiting family and friends. There is no reason why the pattern of previous West Kent visits would have been any different during the summer of 1788, so it is reasonable to believe that Jane and her sister would have spent time at 182 High Street.

If you want to see the house you might already be too late. Warners moved out in 2010 and, as I write, a planning application to demolish the building and replace it with modern flats is being considered.

Henry Austen eventually retired to Tunbridge Wells where he died in 1850. His grave can be found in the small Woodbury Park Cemetery tucked behind St John's Road.

3. Sevenoaks

Jane Austen's godfather, Francis Austen (1698-1791), thought to be by Ozias Humphrey. The original is in the Graves Art gallery, Sheffield.

As we have seen, in 1708 Jane's great grandmother Elizabeth Austen née Weller let the Broadford estate and moved to Sevenoaks (Sennocke she called it), leaving behind her eldest son John Austen V in the care of his father's relations. She took employment as housekeeper to Elijah Fenton, Master of Sevenoaks Grammar School and in return she received free accommodation for herself and reduced tuition fees for her other five boys.

Throughout the years Elizabeth spent in Sevenoaks she kept meticulous accounts of her domestic expenses. A note in her accounts confirms that she remained in contact with her eldest son, John, who was now twenty-three and still living in Horsmonden: 'My son John desires ye Rent at Broadford may be allowed to him as an equivalent for ye Expenses he has been at this Year on his brothers account, & repairs, & for his own part in ye Rents.'

Sevenoaks School where Elizabeth Weller became housekeeper to the headmaster and where Jane Austen's great-uncles were educated.

The Red House built by Thomas Couchman in 1686 and purchased by Jane's great-uncle Francis in 1743.

This fine example of a William and Mary town house still serves today as offices for a firm of solicitors.

Above: The Sevenoaks Preservation Society plaque attached to the railings of The Red House is misleading. Francis Austen, Jane's godfather, was her great-uncle.

In 1720, John married his cousin Mary Stringer. We also learn that in 1714 Francis, her second oldest son, was apprenticed to George Tilden, attorney, of Bedford Row, London, for a premium of £140. It proved to be money very well spent.

Elizabeth herself lived only two years after her youngest son, Stephen, left Sevenoaks School. She died in February 1721 secure in the knowledge that she had given her children the best possible start in life. Her body was brought from Sevenoaks to be buried in the parish church at Tonbridge, although sadly no memorial to this remarkable woman has been found in the church or churchyard.

The following year Francis Austen set up as an attorney in Sevenoaks with a determination to succeed. As Jane's brother Henry later recalled: 'There [at Sevenoaks] my Father's Uncle, old Francis Austen set out in life with £800 and a bundle of pens, as Attorney, & contrived to amass a very large fortune, living most hospitably, and yet buying up all the valuable land round the Town.'

In 1743 Francis purchased The Red House at the top of the town in Sevenoaks. This fine example of a William and Mary town house was built by Thomas Couchman in 1686

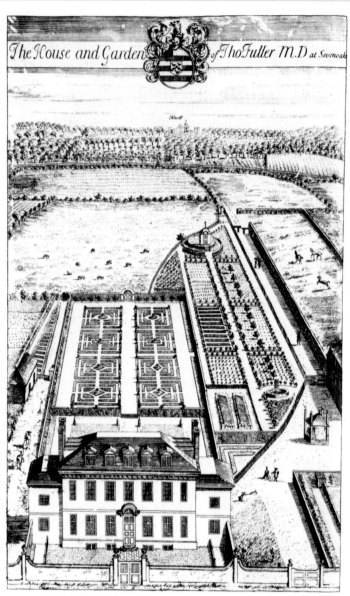

The Red House, Sevenoaks, 1719. The seat of Francis Austen
From Harris's 'History of Kent'

and today still serves as offices for a firm of solicitors.

Over the years Francis Austen became a notable Sevenoaks figure. He was trustee of eleven turnpike trusts and governor of his old school. In 1780, when Jane's brother Henry was nine, he visited The Red House with his parents and left us this description of his great-uncle who at that time was eighty-two:

'All that I remember of him is, that he wore a wig like a Bishop, & a suit of light grey ditto, coat, vest & hose. In his picture over the chimney the coat & vest had a narrow gold lace edging, about half an inch broad, but in my day he had laid aside the gold edging, though he retained a perfect identity of colour, texture make to his life's end – I think he was born in Anne's reign, and was of course a smart man of George the First's. It is a sort of privilege to have seen and conversed with such a model of a hundred years.'

George Austen kept in good contact with his Sevenoaks uncle and patron. In addition to sponsoring his nephew's education, Uncle Francis also acquired for him the living of Deane to add to that of Steventon which had been presented to him by Thomas Knight of Godmersham. The first confirmation we have of Jane visiting Kent is in the summer of 1788 when she was twelve-and-a-half. Accompanied by her parents and her fifteen-year-old sister Cassandra, Jane visited The Red House and Old Uncle Francis who by then was ninety years old but still very capable.

On this trip Jane met many members of the family whom she later called 'our connections in West Kent'. One of these was Philadelphia Walter (known as Philly), the granddaughter of George Austen's mother Rebecca from her first marriage to William Walter. Philly was a great correspondent with Eliza de Feuillide, the daughter of George's sister, Philadelphia Hancock.

The Walter family lived in the nearby village of Seal and Uncle Francis invited them to dinner at The Red House so they could meet their Hampshire cousins. On 23 July 1788, the day after the dinner party, Philly, who was fourteen years older than Jane, wrote to her brother James Walter from Seal:

'Yesterday I began an acquaintance with my 2 female cousins, Austens. My uncle, aunt, Cassandra & Jane arrived at Mr. F. Austen's the day before. We dined with them there. As it is pure Nature to love ourselves, I may be allowed to give the preference to the Eldest who is generally reckoned a most striking resemblance of me in features, complexion & manners…The youngest (Jane) is very like her brother Henry, not at all pretty & very prim, unlike a girl of twelve: but it is a hasty judgment which you will scold me for. My aunt has lost several fore-teeth which makes her look old: my uncle is quite white-haired, but looks vastly well: all in high spirits & disposed to be pleased with each other…Yesterday they all spent the day with us, & the more I see of Cassandra the more I admire [her] – Jane is whimsical and affected.'

The Red House initially had a great deal of land and the curtilage extended to a

Opposite:

Top left: *A copy of Francis Austen's portrait hangs in The Red House entrance hall alongside portraits of his law firm partners.*

Bottom left: *Known as 'The Rice Portrait' because of its family ownership, this painting of a young girl remains a matter of dispute. It is thought by some to be of Jane Austen painted by Ozias Humphrey at the time of the 1788 visit. Others contest its provenance and say it probably dates to 1806.*

Right: *In this 1719 illustration from Harris's* History of Kent *The Red House grounds can be seen to extend to a border with Knole Park.*

The great Elizabethan mansion of Knole.

boundary with Knole Park. Uncle Francis became agent for the Knole estate and parliamentary agent for John Sackville, third Duke of Dorset. It was accepted practice at the time to allow people of sufficient social status access to the great houses. In her journal, Fanny Burney recorded a visit to Knole with her friends the Thrales of whom she said: 'had seen it repeatedly themselves'. This is reflected in *Pride and Prejudice* when Elizabeth Bennett and the Gardiners tour Pemberley and are surprised by the return of Mr Darcy.

From this it seems very likely that the Hampshire Austens would have toured the great house or at the very least walked in the vast deer park during the month they were staying with Uncle Francis, the Duke's agent and closest neighbour.

Kippington in Sevenoaks was home to Uncle Francis's son Francis Motley Austen and his family. It is not known if Jane ever visited this house but she would have had opportunities to do so on her journeys through Kent.

Top: *John Sackville, third Duke of Dorset, to whom Francis Austen was lawyer and agent.*

Above: *Francis Motley Austen, the son of old uncle Francis and his first wife Anne Motley.*

4. Seal and Kemsing

O n the 17 December 1775 Rev'd George Austen sat at his desk in the bow-windowed study of the Steventon rectory and began a letter to his sister-in-law Susannah Walter announcing the birth of his daughter Jane: 'Last night the time came, and without a great deal of warning, everything was soon happily over. We now have another girl, a present plaything for her sister Cassy and a future companion. She is to be Jenny…'

Susannah Walter was the wife of William Hampson Walter, George's half-brother, born to George's mother Rebecca during her first marriage to William Walter. Between 1785 and 1811, William Hampson Walter and his family lived in Church Street, Seal, possibly in the Grey House. The Walters were always on very friendly terms with Jane's family and during the 1788 visit to Sevenoaks the Austens most likely called on their step-relations at nearby Seal.

The Grey House, Church Street, Seal, thought to be the home of William Hampson Walter and his family, half-brother of Rev'd George Austen.

Susannah Walter née Weaver came from Maidstone and bore her husband seven children. The eldest, Weaver, went on to become head boy at Tonbridge School and curate at Penshurst in 1799 where he married two years later.

The youngest child Philadelphia, born in 1761, was closest in age to Jane. Known in the family as Phylly, it is her letter to her brother James that provides us with the first account of Jane's visit to Kent. Phylly married George Whitaker of Pembury late in her life and had no children.

An interesting Austen connection with the village of Seal involves Reverend William Humphrey. He was the younger brother of the artist Ozias Humphrey (he preferred Humphry). William, who was rector of the adjacent village of Kemsing, had married Elizabeth Woodgate the daughter of a prominent Kentish family from Pembury.

Ozias had petitioned the Duke of Dorset to give his brother the additional living at Seal, which was in his gift. The Duke reprimanded Ozias for importuning him over the matter, but having informed him that 'Duke's never forget', he did indeed present William with the living and made him his personal chaplain. In addition to obtaining the patronage of the Duke, Ozias also assisted William financially when he married Elizabeth Woodgate, and he was very fond of his many nephews and nieces.

Ozias travelled to Italy in 1773 with his great friend George Romney, stopping en route at Knole where the Duke of Dorset commissioned several works from him. His stay in Italy lasted until 1777. From 1785 to 1787, he travelled to India, producing many miniatures and sketches and when he returned home to England he stayed with his brother in Seal.

In 1788 Ozias painted a portrait of Madame Bacelli, the Duke's mistress and their illegitimate son, John Frederick Sackville. In a small village like Seal and as the vicar's brother, Ozias was obviously well known to the Walters, and he was actually resident in Seal during the visit of Jane and her family.

When William Hampson Walter died in April 1798 Jane sent the following letter of condolence to her cousin Philadelphia at Seal:

'As Cassandra is at present from home, You must accept from my pen, our sincere Condolance on the melancholy Event which Mrs Humphries Letter announced to my Father this morning.- The loss of so kind & affectionate a Parent, must be a very severe affliction to all his Children, to yourself more especially, as your constant residence with him has given you so much the more constant & intimate Knowledge of his Virtues.- But the very circumstance which at present enhances your loss, must gradually reconcile you to it the better;- the Goodness which made him valuable on Earth, will make him Blessed in Heaven.

This consideration must bring comfort to yourself, to my aunt, & to all his family & friends; & this comfort must be heightened by the consideration of the little Enjoyment he was able to receive from this World for some time past, & of the small degree of pain

*St Clere, the Kentish mansion
owned in Jane's time by Austen
family friend William Evelyn.*

attending his last hours.- I will not press you to write before you would otherwise feel equal to it, but when you can do it without pain, I hope we shall receive from you as good an account of my Aunt & Yourself, as can be expected in these early days of Sorrow.- My Father and Mother join me in every kind wish, & I am my dear Cousin, Yours Affectionately.'

KEMSING

Many years before Jane visited Seal there was already a long standing Austen family connection with William Evelyn, who owned the estate of St Clere which lies a couple of miles to the north-east of Seal. In 1733, the year before William was born, Jane's great Uncle Francis had ownership of an estate at Northfleet which he sold on to William Evelyn's father.

We also know that George Austen's half-brother William Hampson Walter was a friend of William Evelyn and might have been involved in estate duties at St Clere. In George Austen's letter to his sister-in-law, announcing Jane's birth, he goes on to say:

'Let my brother know his friend Mr Evelyn is going to treat us to a plowing match in this neighbourhood on next Tuesday, if the present frost does not continue and prevent it, Kent against Hants for a rump of beef; he sends his own ploughman from St Clair. Does my brother know a Mr Collis, he says he is very well acquainted with him, he visited me to buy some oats for Evelyn's hunters.'

Jane's brother Edward, who was twenty-three at the time when his sister may have visited Seal, was also acquainted with William Evelyn. In addition to the St Clere estate William owned a town house in Bath. In 1799 Jane was on holiday in Bath and noted in a letter to Cassandra that: 'Edward renewed his acquaintance lately with Mr. Evelyn, who lives in the Queen's Parade, and was invited to a family dinner, which I believe at first Elizabeth was rather sorry at his accepting; but yesterday Mrs. Evelyn called on us, and

The impressive entrance hall and staircase at St Clere.

William Hampson Walter may have had management duties on the St Clere estate.

35

The beautiful house of St Clere is now available to hire as a wedding venue.

her manners were so pleasing that we liked the idea of going very much.'

On 19 June 1799 Jane reports that Edward: '…made an important purchase yesterday: no less so than a pair of coach-horses. His friend Mr. Evelyn found them out and recommended them…Their colour is black and their size not large; their price sixty guineas, of which the chair mare was taken as fifteen – but this is of course to be a secret.'

In 1801 when the Austens came to live permanently in Bath they socialised with the Evelyns. On 26 May Jane wrote to Cassandra: 'I assure you in spite of what I might chuse to insinuate in a former letter, that I have seen very little of Mr Evelyn since my coming here; I met him this morning for only the 4th time, & as to my anecdote about Sidney Gardens, I made the most of the story because it came in to advantage, but in fact he only asked me whether I were to be at Sidney Gardens in the evening or not.'

With all this inter-connection with the Evelyns it seems more than possible that the Austen family would have taken the opportunity to visit St Clere during the summer of 1788. This beautiful house is now available to hire as a wedding venue.

5. Bromley

During Jane Austen's lifetime three great roads traversed Kent. The northerly route from London crossed the River Darenth at Dartford then the River Medway at Rochester before heading for Canterbury via Faversham and is detailed in the following chapter.

The central route, went through Maidstone and Ashford to end at Hythe. The most southerly road headed south out of London passing over the River Ravensbourne at Lewisham Bridge and through Bromley which, at that time, was a country town, only becoming a part of Greater London from 1965.

Over a period of nineteen years from 1794 to 1813, Jane made at least ten trips across Kent on extended visits to family and friends. Her journeys were made in stages of around 10 to 12 miles from one inn to another where coach horses could be changed and refreshment and accommodation was available.

In English towns coaching inns were generally the most prominent and numerous of the buildings. Every town in the country had at least one inn but they varied greatly and this was sometimes a factor in Jane's choice of route.

The views on coach travel put forward by Lady Catherine de Bourgh in *Pride & Prejudice*, are interesting regarding young women travelling post (on a stage coach) unescorted:

'Lady Catherine seemed resigned. Mrs. Collins, you must send a servant with them. You know I always speak my mind, and I cannot bear the idea of two young women travelling post by themselves. It is highly improper. You must contrive to send somebody. I have the greatest dislike in the world to that sort of thing. Young women should always be properly guarded and attended, according to their situation in life. When my niece Georgiana went to Ramsgate last summer, I made a point of her having two men-servants go with her.'

This highlights the fact that Jane herself was highly dependent on her father or brothers to escort her, her sister or their mother to any place beyond walking distance from their home. No respectable lady would ever travel by herself. In *Pride and Prejudice*, Elizabeth Bennet is able to insist on leaving Rosings as originally planned because her uncle's manservant will be there to escort her and Maria Lucas back to London; after changing from the de Bourgh carriage to a hired private coach at a nearby inn.

The type of private hire vehicle Jane used most over the years was the 'post-chaise'. Painted bright yellow like a New York cab, these small carriages were drawn by two

The original seventeenth-century posting house that Jane knew was demolished in 1897. Photograph courtesy of Bromley Library

horses with the postilion riding one of the pair. We learn that Lady Catherine's home at Rosings Park is about 10 miles from Bromley but her reputation was obviously widely known.

'Oh! Your uncle! He keeps a man-servant, does he? I am very glad you have somebody who thinks of these things. Where shall you change horses? Oh! Bromley, of course. If you mention my name at the Bell, you will be attended to.'

The original seventeenth-century posting house that Jane knew and featured in *Pride and Prejudice* was demolished in 1897. At the end of the eighteenth century, two coaches a day ran return trips from here to London. The building we see today was built in 1898 from a design by Ernest Newton, an important Arts and Crafts movement architect. His concept was to create three separate buildings that could be seen as a whole, mirroring the façade of the original inn.

The present day Grade II listed Royal Bell stands on the original site in Bromley High Street, just off the market square. It has been closed for several years after being home to a succession of failed pubs. There is now a local action group campaigning and fund-raising to preserve the building and convert it to a community centre and performing arts venue with a coffee shop, pub and gallery incorporating a studio with rehearsal spaces.

A local action group is campaigning and fund raising to preserve the building for community use.

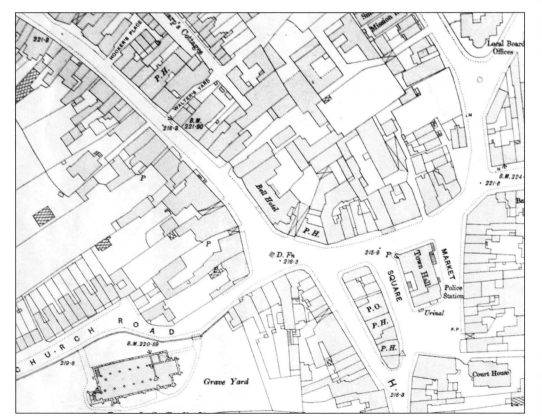

The Grade II listed Royal Bell stands in Bromley High Street, just off the market square.
Map courtesy of Bromley Library

6. Westerham and Chevening

The George & Dragon, one of Westerham's great coaching inns Jane would have known.

The small town of Westerham is strategically placed against the background of Jane's Kentish journeys. It is positioned at the point where the road south from London through Bromley intersects with the east/west route from Hampshire through Surrey into Kent.

This situation and the fact that Jane chose it as a named location suggest it is somewhere she knew fairly well. On the east/west route she would have crossed the Kentish border just before arriving at Westerham where two of the great coaching inns she would have known, The George & Dragon and The Kings Arms, still thrive today.

As long as Jane Austen's novels are read, people will continue to play the delicious game of trying to identify the 'originals' of the fictional houses in which she placed her characters. In *Pride and Prejudice* Jane provides clues to the location of Rosings Park and the adjoining Hunsford Parsonage; the homes of Lady Catherine de Bourgh and Rev'd Collins.

First she tells us that Rosings lay in the village of Hunsford near Westerham, a convenient distance from London and nearly 50 miles from Longbourn, the Hertfordshire home of the Bennet family. Records of journeys between Longbourn and Hunsford, with pauses made in London at the home of Mr and Mrs Gardiner in Gracechurch Street, reveal that the drive from Hunsford to the Gardiners was completed within four hours, changing horses at The Bell in Bromley.

From Gracechurch Street, journeying north to the unnamed town near Longbourn where the travellers were met by Mr Bennet's carriage was a distance of 24 miles. We can conclude from this that Rosings also lay some 24 miles from London to the south, near Westerham, on a route through Bromley which would be roughly half way. This is a route that Jane knew well from travelling to East Kent from her brother Henry's London house.

The most direct route from Hampshire to East Kent would have taken her through Guildford, Reigate, and Westerham, over the Sundridge Cross by Chevening and onwards via Borough Green and Maidstone. At one time a section of this road actually ran through Chevening Park.

David Waldron-Smithers, in his 1981 book *Jane Austen in Kent* puts forward a proposal that Chevening Park was Jane's model for Rosings Park, which he claims she visited in 1796 when Grizel, the Dowager Lady Stanhope, was living at the Dower House. Certainly many of the features of Chevening House and estate fit, or can be made to fit Jane's descriptions, but other Austen scholars dispute the claim and say it is more likely that

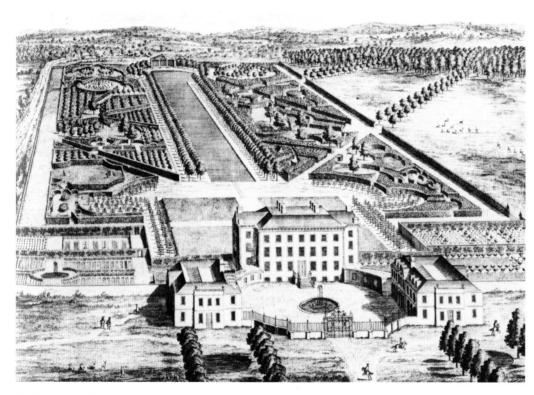

In Jane's time Chevening House was the seat of the Stanhopes.

Pride and Prejudice was written in the mid-1790s.

Lady Catherine de Bourgh, both physically and temperamentally, bears many resemblances to the Dowager Lady Stanhope who was wife of the second earl and mother of the third. She would have been in her seventies in the 1790s. Her personality certainly sounds similar to Lady Catherine. She lived to be ninety-two, and the second earl said she was a most determined woman and a rather fierce old lady who dominated his life and that of his descendants.

Nigel Nicholson in his 1991 book *The World of Jane Austen* admits that Chevening has some resemblance with Rosings but concludes that houses like the one described by Rev'd Collins as: 'a handsome modern building, well situated on rising ground' could be found in many parts of England. In Jane Austen's day the house would have been about 165 years old, but it had just undergone extensive renovation which might have rendered it as handsome and modern.

The design of Chevening, built in 1620 in the English Renaissance style, was influenced by Inigo Jones. The house and estate were bought in 1717 by Major General

Since 1980, Chevening House has been the official residence of Britain's Foreign Secretary.

*Members of the public enjoy the
maze at Chevening during the
opening of the grounds on
National Gardens Day.*

James Stanhope, who the following year became the first Earl Stanhope. Lord Stanhope's family, the Lennards, employed George Austen's Uncle Francis as their solicitor during the latter third of the eighteenth century.

Old Francis himself owned property in and around Chevening, and may well have taken his grand-nieces over some of this ground during their first visit to Kent in 1788 and it is likely that Jane and some of her close family visited it on other occasions. If nothing else, Jane would have passed close by in later years on visits to Godmersham. She certainly had the opportunity to know the Westerham and Chevening area well.

John Austen, son of Francis Motley Austen, became Rector of Chevening in 1813, the year that Jane published *Pride and Prejudice*, her most famous novel.

Chevening remained the seat of the Stanhopes for two hundred and fifty years. In 1967, on the death without issue of the seventh Earl, the estate was bequeathed to the nation, with the condition that only someone of royal lineage, or the Prime Minister or a cabinet minister should live there.

It was originally intended to become the residence of Prince Charles, but he decided to live at Highgrove in Gloucestershire. Therefore from 1980, Chevening became the official residence of the Foreign Secretary, starting with Lord Carrington.

At the time of writing England has a coalition government elected in 2010, the house therefore is currently shared between Philip Hammond, Foreign Secretary, and Nick Clegg, Deputy Prime Minister. The gardens are open annually under the National Gardens Scheme.

*Grizel, Dowager Lady Stanhope
who shared personality
characteristics with Lady
Catherine de Bourgh.*

7. Dartford

The Kentish road Jane knew best is our present day A2 which runs for 71 miles from London to Dover. The section she was most familiar with was the 41 miles from Dartford to Canterbury, passing through Rochester, Sittingbourne and Ospringe.

This most ancient of roads, known as Watling Street, began life as a Celtic grassy trackway which was later paved by the Romans and straightened to follow a more direct course. After fording the Thames at Westminster, the route crossed the River Cray and the River Darent at Crayford and Dartford respectively. The Romans constructed the first bridge over the River Medway at Rochester.

This illustration by Turner shows Dartford High Street much as Jane would have known it. The first inn on the left is The Bulls Head.

Opposite: The Royal Victoria & Bull in Dartford High Street is the last remaining of the inns that Jane would have known.

Opposite, clockwise
from top left:
*Jane stayed at The Bull &
George in 1788. It was
demolished in 1981.*

*All that remains now of The
Bull's Head shown in the
picture by Turner.*

*This modern Boots Pharmacy
stands on the site of The Bull
& George.*

*Dartford Borough Council is
proud of its Jane Austen
connection.*

Following the murder of Thomas Becket at Canterbury in 1170, people began journeying from Southwark to the shrine of the saint in the Cathedral. At the end of the fourteenth century Geoffrey Chaucer described the scene in his *Canterbury Tales*, featuring a group of storytelling pilgrims. The number of hostels along the route steadily increased to meet the needs of the growing numbers of travellers and by the seventeenth century these had been augmented by numerous inns.

Jane often chose this route when travelling from Hampshire to Godmersham. Although it was a longer way round compared with the more central route through Sevenoaks, Maidstone and Ashford it was ultimately faster and the available accommodation was generally better.

In 1809, when going into Kent from Great Bookham, Surrey, the home of her mother's relatives the Cookes, Jane proposed to travel north through Croydon and sleep at Dartford as: 'There certainly does seem no convenient resting place on the other road.' By which she presumably meant the road through Sevenoaks and Maidstone.

In eighteenth-century towns, inns were often very close together, sometimes next door to one another. Dartford inns included The Hart, The Bell, The King's Inn or Crown, The Swan, The Cock-on-the-Hoop, Le Maiden Head and The Saracen's Head. In addition to these there were three with the word Bull in their title; The Bull (later the Royal Victoria & Bull), The Bull & George and The Bull's Head.

Jane's letters give us several accounts of her excursions along the Dover Road, generally with more details of her homeward journeys. The following example is from a letter written to Cassandra from Dartford on Wednesday 24 October 1788. It is headed the 'Bull & George' which stood on the southern side of the High Street.

'You have already heard from Daniel, I conclude, in what excellent time we reached and quitted Sittingbourne, and how very well my mother bore her journey thither. I am now able to send you a continuation of the same good account of her. She was very little fatigued on her arrival at this place, has been refreshed by a comfortable dinner, and now seems quite stout. It wanted five minutes of twelve when we left Sittingbourne, from whence we had a famous pair of horses, which took us to Rochester in an hour and a quarter; the postboy seemed determined to show my mother that Kentish drivers were not always tedious, and really drove as fast as *Cax*.

Our next stage was not quite so expeditiously performed; the road was heavy and our horses very indifferent. However, we were in such good time, and my mother bore her journey so well, that expedition was of little importance to us; and as it was, we were very little more than two hours and a half coming hither, and it was scarcely past four when we stopped at the inn.

We have got apartments up two pair of stairs, as we could not be otherwise accommodated with a sitting-room and bed-chambers on the same floor, which we

JANE AUSTEN
1775 - 1817
Noted Novelist
Jane Austen stayed at the former inn on this site, The Bull and George, when travelling to visit her brother in Canterbury.

wished to be. We have one double-bedded and one single-bedded room; in the former my mother and I are to sleep. I shall leave you to guess who is to occupy the other. We sate down to dinner a little after five, and had some beefsteaks and a boiled fowl, but no oyster sauce.

I should have begun my letter soon after our arrival but for a little adventure which prevented me. After we had been here a quarter of an hour it was discovered that my writing and dressing boxes had been by accident put into a chaise which was just packing off as we came in, and were driven away towards Gravesend in their way to the West Indies. No part of my property could have been such a prize before, for in my writing-box was all my worldly wealth, £7, and my dear Harry's deputation. Mr. Nottley immediately despatched a man and horse after the chaise, and in half an hour's time I had the pleasure of being as rich as ever; they were got about two or three miles off.

My day's journey has been pleasanter in every respect than I expected. I have been very little crowded and by no means unhappy. Your watchfulness with regard to the weather on our accounts was very kind and very effectual. We had one heavy shower on leaving Sittingbourne, but afterwards the clouds cleared away, and we had a very bright *chrystal* afternoon.

My father is now reading the "Midnight Bell," which he has got from the library, and mother sitting by the fire. Our route to-morrow is not determined. We have none of us much inclination for London, and if Mr. Nottley will give us leave, I think we shall go to Staines through Croydon and Kingston, which will be much pleasanter than any other way; but he is decidedly for Clapham and Battersea. God bless you all!

Yours affectionately,

J. A.'

Towards the end of its life as an inn, the ground floor of The Bull & George was converted for retail use and occupied by Mr Edwards' chemist shop. The building was demolished in 1981 and a modern Boots store now occupies the site. Bull as part of an inn name often meant the establishment had ecclesiastical origins. The use derives from Bulla, a seal issued by the Pope to a religious house providing lodging for their visitors and for travellers.

This was the case with another Dartford inn The Royal Victoria & Bull, known simply in Jane's time as the Bull. The original inn on this site is mentioned in the Priory Rental of 1508 as 'le Hole Bull'. In the eighteenth-century it was Dartford's premier inn and famous on the Dover Road. Jane would have been aware of the inn's reputation and would almost certainly have stayed here on occasion. Perhaps her preferred inn was full when she stayed at The Bull & George and had to contend with 'apartments up two pair of stairs'?

The galleried courtyard of The Royal Victoria & Bull has been covered with a glass roof where, until recently, an original London/Dartford stage coach was displayed.

8. Rochester and Sittingbourne

The section in the Dartford letter where Jane refers to the speedy postboy and the 'famous pair of horses', taking her and her mother from Sittingbourne to Rochester in an hour and a quarter, suggests they were travelling in a post-chaise rather than the common stage. Stage coaches were regulated by the minute with regard to stops but post-chaise carriages were for private hire, so passengers could dictate their own timetable.

With this in mind, it would be reasonable to think that on one of her journeys through Rochester Jane would have made time to visit the Cathedral. Her father, Rev'd George Austen, was ordained as a deacon at Christ Church Oxford in March 1754 and as a priest in May the following year, when he was twenty-four. This second ceremony took place in Rochester Cathedral, the second oldest cathedral in the land after Canterbury.

In another letter, this time written to Cassandra on 15 June 1808, Jane gives us a further

The Royal Victoria & Bull Inn which Jane would have known featured later in Pickwick Papers *and* Great Expectations *by Charles Dickens.*

Rochester Cathedral where Jane's father, the Rev'd George Austen, was ordained as a priest in 1754.

On her coach journeys through Kent Jane would have passed close by Rochester Cathedral and it seems more than likely she would have made time for a visit.

description of a journey along the Dover Road. On this occasion she was travelling from the Bath Hotel in London's Arlington Street with a family party including her nephew James, her niece Caroline, her sister-in-law Mary Lloyd Austen plus a maidservant, Mary Smallbone.

Three of Jane's brothers, Henry, James and Edward, were involved in the arrangements. Henry had taken Jane early in the morning to the hotel to meet the party. They were to travel in James's new carriage while Henry went ahead on a stage coach. We learn that Mary Austen shopped briefly in Sittingbourne High Street for gloves and that Edward had sent his servant to meet the party at the George Inn:

'Where shall I begin? Which of all my important nothings shall I tell you first? At half after seven yesterday morning Henry saw us into our own carriage, and we drove away from the Bath Hotel; which, by-the-bye, had been found most uncomfortable quarters – very dirty, very noisy, and very ill-provided. James began his journey by the coach at five. Our first eight miles were hot; Deptford Hill brought to my mind our hot journey into Kent fourteen years ago*; but after Blackheath we suffered nothing, and as the day advanced it grew quite cool. At Dartford, which we reached within the two hours and three-quarters, we went to the Bull, the same inn at which we breakfasted in that said journey, and on the present occasion had about the same bad butter.

At half-past ten we were again off, and, travelling on without any adventure reached Sittingbourne by three. Daniel was watching for us at the door of the George, and I was acknowledged very kindly by Mr. and Mrs. Marshall, to the latter of whom I devoted my conversation, while Mary went out to buy some gloves. A few minutes, of course, did for Sittingbourne; and so off we drove, drove, drove, and by six o'clock were at Godmersham'.

Sittingbourne is 15 miles from Godmersham. A map of 1769 shows it as a small town bordering Watling Street. The High Street in Jane's time consisted largely of inns and there would have been up to a dozen of them. Several still exist today though much altered. The most famous inn in Sittingbourne was the Red Lion, known formerly as The Lyon where parts of the Banqueting Hall have survived.

The old coaching inn yard at the Red Lion, Sittingbourne.

Henry V stopped here on his return from the battle of Agincourt in 1415 and Henry VIII was in the town in 1522 and again in 1532. Other inns that Jane would have known include The Bull, The George and The Rose built in 1708. In 1790 John Byng (later Viscount Torrington) stopped here during his leisurely tour of Kent: 'I jogg'd on my slow pace to Sittingbourne, where I dined very comfortably at the Rose Inn. The apartments are good, but the stabling very bad.' The Rose, at 50 High Street, is no longer an inn but the building still exists with the ground floor converted to shops.

*This means that Jane and Cassandra had also undertaken this journey in the summer of 1794. No letters exist because the sisters were together.

9. Ospringe, Norton and Provender

OSPRINGE

The village of Ospringe lies on the main Dover Road a mile south of Faversham where a remarkable feature bearing witness to the history of this ancient highway can be seen. Jane would have been familiar with the Maison Dieu or 'Gods House'; a hostel, monastery and Royal lodge combined, commissioned by Henry III in 1234. The early sixteenth-century timber-framed building we see today incorporates fragments of the thirteenth-century hospital and shelter for pilgrims.

The Maison Dieu or 'Gods House' in Ospringe that would have been a familiar sight to Jane is now open as a tourist attraction.

The Red Lion, the principal inn in Ospringe in Jane's time, has been converted for residential use.

Here hospitality was offered to poor and needy travellers as well as to the highest in the land. There was a chamber inside which was then called Camera Regis, or the King's Chamber in which the king used to repose when he passed this way. Some antiquaries have identified Ospringe as the site of the Roman station of Durolevum and there are displays in the Maison Dieu of Roman artefacts discovered in graves around the village.

When Jane travelled this way, her carriage would have passed through the same water splash that soothed the feet of Chaucer's Canterbury-bound pilgrims. A little stream flowed across the highway here and no one thought it worthwhile bridging.

Jane mentions Ospringe in four of her letters. Her mother was often unwell and suffered from travel sickness. This comment appears in Jane's letter written at the Bull & George when she tells Cassandra: 'My mother took some of her bitters at Ospringe, and some more at Rochester, and she ate some bread several times.' In Jane's time the principal inn at Ospringe was the Red Lion which has now been converted for residential use.

In a letter written from Steventon on 21 January 1799 Jane displays her knowledge of East Kent. Her youngest sailor brother Charles was to join his ship the *Tamar* which was anchored in the Downs – an area of sand ridges off the coast at Deal:

> 'Charles leaves us to-night. The "Tamar" is in the Downs, and Mr. Daysh advises him to join her there directly, as there is no chance of her going to the westward. Charles does not approve of this at all, and will not be much grieved if he should be too late for her before she sails, as he may then hope to get into a better station. He attempted to go to town last night, and got as far on his road thither as Dean Gate; but both the coaches were full, and we had the pleasure of seeing him back again. He will call on Daysh to-morrow to know whether the "Tamar" has sailed or not, and if she is still at the Downs he will proceed in one of the night coaches to Deal. I want to go with him, that I may explain the country to him properly between Canterbury and Rowling, but the unpleasantness of returning by myself deters me. I should like to go as far as Ospringe with him very much indeed, that I might surprise you at Godmersham'.

Norton Court lodge.

NORTON

In Jane Austen's time there were no envelopes or postage stamps and it was the recipient of the letter who paid for the cost of delivery. Letters were written on large sheets of paper with room left for the address. The sheet was then folded in four and sealed with wax. The cost of delivery was based on the number of sheets and distance conveyed. In 1812 the cost to deliver a single sheet varied between four and seventeen old pence.

One way to avoid the cost, and something Jane did when she could, was to persuade a Member of Parliament, who had the privilege of sending letters free of charge, to frank a letter for her. MPs could give a friend a blank sheet of paper (franked) or signed by them which could then be used to send a private letter which would be received free of charge.

The seventeenth-century service wing to the original Norton Court mansion.

Stephen Rumbold Lushington of whom Jane said: 'I like him very much... I am rather in love with him. I dare say he is ambitious and insincere.'

Jane acknowledges this accepted fraud in *Mansfield Park* when Edmund Bertram assures the astonished Fanny Price that her first letter to her brother will be franked by her otherwise upright uncle, Sir Thomas Bertram.

In Hampshire Jane cultivated the friendship of William John Chute MP, and in Kent she turned to Stephen Rumbold Lushington whom she met on occasion at Godmersham. Lushington, almost the same age as Jane, was MP for Canterbury and lived here at Norton Court. On the address panel of Jane's letter written to Cassandra from Godmersham on 14 October 1813 her Parliamentary contact has written the word 'Free' and signed R. Lushington.

In the letter Jane told Cassandra: 'I like him very much. I am sure he is clever, and a man of taste. He got a volume of Milton last night, and spoke of it with warmth. He is quite an M.P., very smiling, with an exceeding good address and readiness of language. I am rather in love with him. I dare say he is ambitious and insincere. He puts me in mind of Mr Dundas. He has a wide smiling mouth, and very good teeth, and something of the same complexion and nose.'

It seems that Jane's niece Fanny Knight was also rather taken with Mr Lushington because she recorded this note in her pocket book: 'Mr Lushington sang. He has a lovely voice, and is quite delightful.' One of Lushington's eight children, Mary Ann, married James Wildman of Chilham Castle, who had formerly courted Fanny Knight.

The Norton estate lies south of the A2, between Sittingbourne and Faversham. The house was originally built in 1625 for the Milles family. The seventeenth-century building we see today was a service wing to the original mansion which was destroyed by fire in 1966. The ten acre garden within parkland setting is open for charity on certain days under the National Gardens Scheme.

This display in Canterbury Museum shows some of the arms and armour, as well as a large number of animal skins, collected by Lushington when he served as Governor of Madras.

Above: *The memorial to Stephen Rumbold Lushington in St Mary's church.*

Left: *St Mary's 'the Church in the Orchard' adjacent to Norton Court.*

PROVENDER

This beautiful sixteenth-century half-timbered house which stands a short distance from Norton Court, becomes crucially important in our understanding of Jane Austen's life story. Edward Knatchbull, 8th Baronet of Mersham le Hatch married Mary Hugessen of Provender. In 1806, Edward and Mary's son, Edward Knatchbull-Hugessen, married Annabella Christiana Honeywood and the couple lived in Provender where they had six children.

The beautiful house of Provender is being slowly and carefully restored by the present owner Princess Olga Romanoff.

It was at Provender in 1883 that Lord Brabourne discovered a square box containing 'the letters from Jane and Cassandra Austen, treasured by the mother who had loved both'.

Guided tours of Provender are available as well as facilities for wedding functions, lunches, dinners and society events.

Edward Knatchbull-Hugessen, whose son became the 9th Baronet and the first Lord Brabourne, was six years younger than Jane. In a letter of 26 June 1808 Jane records meeting him in Canterbury at the White Friars home of Mrs Knight:

'Mr. Knatchbull, from Provender, was at the W. Friars when we arrived, and stayed dinner, which, with Harriot, who came, as you may suppose, in a great hurry, ten minutes after the time, made our number six. Mr. K. went away early… Mrs. C. Knatchbull and I breakfasted tête-à-tête the next day, for her husband was gone to Mr. Toke's, and Mrs. Knight had a sad headache which kept her in bed.'

There is no specific reference to Jane visiting Norton Court or Provender but she was back in Kent in 1809 and again in 1813 so she would have had plenty of opportunities and incentives for doing so.

Annabella Honeywood died in 1814 and in 1820, three years after Jane's death, Edward Knatchbull-Hugessen married Jane's beloved niece Fanny Knight. Although Edward was a widower, twelve years older than Fanny and with six children, it appears

Fanny Knight painted by Cassandra. As Lady Knatchbull, Fanny lived on at Provender and inherited her Aunt Jane's letters.

to have been an equitable marriage and Fanny produced nine more children for the baronet.

After Edward died in 1849 Fanny, as Lady Knatchbull, lived on at Provender for another thirty-three years, fretting that the house with its thirty rooms would be inadequate for her seven family members and twelve servants. Fanny died in 1882 at the age of eighty-nine.

Fanny's eldest son, Lord Brabourne, who edited the first edition of Jane Austen's letters, lived at Provender. In 1883 he discovered a square box containing 'the letters from Jane and Cassandra Austen, treasured by the mother who had loved both' and the world has been the richer ever since. He wrote:

'On my mother's death, in December, 1882, all her papers came into my possession, and I not only found the original copy of "Lady Susan" – in Jane Austen's own hand-writing – among the other books in the Provender library, but a square box full of letters, fastened up carefully in separate packets, each of which was endorsed 'For Lady Knatchbull,' in the handwriting of my great-aunt, Cassandra Austen, and with which was a paper endorsed, in my mother's handwriting, "Letters from my dear Aunt Jane Austen, and two from Aunt Cassandra after her decease," which paper contained the letters written to my mother herself.

The box itself had been endorsed by my mother as follows: "Letters from Aunt Jane to Aunt Cassandra at different periods of her life – a few to me – and some from Aunt Cassandra to me after At. Jane's death". This endorsement bears the date August, 1856, and was probably made the last time my mother looked at the letters.'

Provender is now the home of Princess Olga Romanoff, daughter of Prince Andrew Romanoff who was the eldest nephew of the Tsar Nicholas II of Russia. The Knatchbull-Hugessens rented the house to Princess Olga's maternal great-grandmother in 1890, and sold it at auction in 1912 to her Finnish grandmother Sylvia McDougall, born Borgström in Helsinki.

During the Second World War, Provender was requisitioned, and was one of Field Marshall Montgomery's Headquarters. Prince Andrew Romanoff married Sylvia's daughter Nadine in 1942 and after the War Provender was returned to them. Under the care of Princess Olga Romanoff, Provender is slowly and carefully being restored with further works ongoing. Guided tours are available as well as facilities for wedding functions, lunches, dinners and society events.

10. Rowling and Goodnestone

ROWLING

Jane's experience of East Kent was the result of family connections through her father's patron Thomas Knight who had presented Rev'd George Austen the living of Steventon. Thomas was the descendent of the fourth John Austen of Horsmonden and owned the Hampshire estates of Steventon and Chawton as well as Godmersham in Kent, which later passed to his son Thomas Knight II.

In 1799 Thomas junior married Catherine Knatchbull whose family had owned the impressive estate at Mersham-le-Hatch for over three-hundred years. Catherine was the daughter of Wadham Knatchbull, a younger son of the family and Rector of Chilham. When Thomas and Catherine married she was twenty-six and he was almost twenty years her senior.

For their honeymoon they made a tour of the family estates and when calling on the Austens at Steventon were so taken with Jane's brother Edward that they asked if the young lad could accompany them for the rest of the trip. The following summer a letter arrived from the Knights asking if little Edward might be allowed to spend what was to be the first of several holidays with them at Godmersham.

After four years of marriage, there was no sign that the Knights were to have a child and consequently no forthcoming heir to the Godmersham and Chawton estates. In the course of time the Knights offered to adopt Edward as their heir and it proved to be an admirable arrangement for all concerned.

In 1791 Edward married Elizabeth Bridges, one of the daughters of Sir Brook Bridges from the neighbouring estate of Goodnestone (pronounced Gunston). Elizabeth was the third daughter in a family of thirteen children and she had eleven children of her own with Edward. Before inheriting Goodnestone, he and Elizabeth lived in a small manor house on the estate called Rowling, only a mile from Goodnestone Park.

It is to this house in 1794 that Jane came to stay with her brother and sister-in-law on her first visit to East Kent. At Rowling Jane began the first versions of *Sense and Sensibility* and *Northanger Abbey*. Elizabeth had given birth to her first baby the previous year. This daughter, christened Fanny Catherine was to become one of Jane's favourite nieces. There was also a new baby in the house, a boy born three months before the visit, christened Edward after his father.

In August 1796 Jane travelled to Rowling via London in the company of brothers

On 27 December 1791, Jane's brother Edward married Elizabeth Bridges, one of the daughters of Sir Brook Bridges from Goodnestone Park.

Edward and Elizabeth spent the first years of their marriage at Rowling, a small manor house on the Goodnestone estate.

Francis and Edward, who had been away from home on business. Brother Henry was already at Rowling. As Cassandra was not with the party we get a little flurry of letters from which we learn that Jane was busy with her writing, needlework, playing the piano and amusing the young children.

She tells Cassandra she: '…opened the ball with Edward Bridges' [her sister-in-law's younger brother]. At that time Jane was twenty-one and young Edward was seventeen. Edward was taken with Jane and maintained an affection for her for well over a decade. By the time he was twenty-six he was taking pains to recommend himself to her. In 1805 during a visit to Godmersham, Jane wrote to Cassandra: '[W]e could not begin dinner till six. We were agreeably surprised by Edward Bridges's company to it… It is impossible to do justice to the hospitality of his attentions towards me; he made a point of ordering toasted cheese for supper entirely on my account.'

Deirdre Le Faye, in *Jane Austen: A Family Record*, says: 'It seems possible that Edward Bridges (who became a clergyman, though his father was a baronet) proposed or attempted to propose to Jane during her 1808 visit to Godmersham … a proposal which she had no difficulty in politely rejecting.'

The flirtation became the inspiration for the 2007 BBC drama film *Miss Austen Regrets* staring Olivia Williams as Jane and Hugh Bonneville as The Rev'd Brook Edward Bridges, brother-in-law of Edward Austen. Writer Gwyneth Hughes generally tried to stay close to the few facts we have about Jane's life but it was mostly speculation. I can't help thinking that Jane herself would find it all very amusing – I certainly did.

GOODNESTONE

Holy Cross church, on the Goodnestone estate, witnessed the double wedding of Edward Austen and Elizabeth Bridges and her sister Sophia who married William Deedes of Sandling. This was perhaps the inspiration for the double wedding of Lizzie and Jane

This 1719 illustration of Goodnestone from Harris's History of Kent *shows the mansion before a third storey was added.*

Goodnestone has been the home of Lord FitzWalter's family for over three-hundred years.

Bennet in *Pride and Prejudice* for 'The day on which Mrs Bennet got rid of her two eldest daughters…'

Edward and Elizabeth spent the first years of their marriage living at Rowling and their first four children were born there. When Jane visited them, she was often entertained at Goodnestone with dinners and dances.

Where Rowling is attractively compact, Goodnestone is large and imposing. It was built in 1704 by the first Bridges 'FitzWalter' Baronet and was later heightened by the addition of an extra storey without spoiling its proportions. It has been the home of Lord FitzWalter's family for over three-hundred years.

In Jane's letters of this time we are introduced to some of the East Kent neighbours and begin to have an insight into the social scene. From Rowling on Monday 5 September she wrote:

'We were at a ball on Saturday, I assure you. We dined at Goodnestone, and in the evening danced two country-dances and the Boulangeries. I opened the ball with Edward Bridges; the other couples were Lewis Cage and Harriet [Bridges], Frank

Holy Cross church, seen from the garden of Goodnestone, witnessed the double wedding of Edward Austen and Elizabeth Bridges and her sister Sophia who married William Deedes.

The gardens at Goodnestone Park are now among the most admired in the country and are open to the public for most of the year.

In August 1805 Jane stayed here in the Dower House. Her bedroom was probably the one under the right hand dormer window.

[Jane's brother] and Louisa [Bridges], Fanny and George [Cage]. Elizabeth [Austen née Bridges] played one country-dance, Lady Bridges the other, which she made Henry [Jane's brother] dance with her, and Miss Finch [from Eastwell Park] played the Boulangeries… We supped there, and walked home at night under the shade of two umbrellas.'

A low wall divides Goodnestone from its Dower House which Jane knew as Goodnestone Farm. Lady Bridges lived here in her widowhood with her unmarried daughters and orphaned grand-daughters, the Cages. Although Jane was entertained at Goodnestone House, we do not know for certain that she ever slept there. However, she did spend nights in the Dower House and her bedroom was probably the one under the right hand dormer window.

In August 1805 she was staying here and making use of Lady Bridges own bedroom where she found the shelves in a state of great disorder and wrote: 'what a treat for my mother to arrange them'. In this letter written on Friday 30 August she reported:

'We have walked to Rowling on each of the two last days after dinner, and very great was my pleasure in going over the house and grounds. We have also found time to visit all the principal walks of this place, except the walk round the top of the park, which we shall accomplish probably to-day.'

In 1955, when the twenty-first Lord FitzWalter inherited the estate and moved into the house with his young family Goodnestone was not in the best repair. The elegant Queen Anne mansion had been occupied by the Armed Forces during the Second World War and then let to a tenant. Four years later a fire broke out which removed the roof, gutted the top two floors and caused serious damage to the main rooms on the ground floor, though the furniture and paintings were rescued.

Rather than demolishing the remains of the house which had been built by an ancestor and building a 'sensible' modern house (as he was advised), Lord FitzWalter carefully reconstructed the property over the next eighteen months. It became a source of quiet pride to him when the house celebrated its 300th anniversary. Perhaps the most notable achievement of Brook and Margaret FitzWalter was the restoration and development of the gardens at Goodnestone Park, which are now among the most admired in the country and are open to the public for most of the year.

Brook FitzWalter died in October 2004 and is survived by his wife and five sons. The eldest, Julian, born in 1952, succeeded as the twenty-second Lord FitzWalter and has plans underway for further restoration of the house incorporating a number of self-catering apartments.

If you visit the garden you can be fairly sure to meet Lady FitzWalter, formerly Margaret Deedes, the youngest sister of Lord Deedes of Saltwood Castle.

11. Godmersham

In November 1797, having eventually inherited the estate of Godmersham, Edward Austen and his family moved from Rowling to the big house. Thereafter his brothers and sisters were welcome guests at the mansion. Jane was a regular visitor over a period of fifteen years and Godmersham became more closely connected with her life and work than any other surviving house with the exception of Chawton Cottage in Hampshire.

Prolonged visits to Godmersham presented Jane with golden opportunities to observe life in a great house and provided her with authentic background material. There can be little doubt she derived many ideas for her fictional characters and settings from gatherings at Godmersham and the expeditions she made to neighbouring houses. Some of the people and places she depicts may well have had their counterparts in this little country parish of two-hundred years ago. Indeed, Godmersham may well have been the model for *Mansfield Park*.

Godmersham lies fairly low in a broad valley of the River Stour about 8 miles south-west of Canterbury between Wye and Chilham. The house, a long, low red-brick building, is one of the loveliest to survive from the early part of the eighteenth century. It was built around 1732 by Thomas Knight, father of Edward Austen's benefactor. The wings were added in the 1770s; one for the kitchens the other for the great library.

Godmersham looks north to the Pilgrims' Way and south across the river to a long ridge of the Downs. The illustration from Edward Hasted's *History of the County of Kent* shows the setting much as it would have appeared to Jane. We can easily imagine her riding through the deer park in a post-chaise with one of her brothers following on horseback. It was not until later that the road from Ashford to Canterbury (the present A28) was moved away from the house to the river's far bank.

In *Pride and Prejudice* Jane gives a description of Pemberley seen through Elizabeth Bennet's eyes: 'Every disposition of the ground was good; and she looked on the whole scene, the river, the trees scattered on its banks and the winding of the valley with delight.' On arriving in

Below left: Thomas Knight II, Edward's adoptive father, inherited the estates of Godmersham, Steventon and Chawton in 1781.

Below right: Catherine Knight (née Knatchbull), Edward's adoptive mother, married Thomas Knight II in 1779.

Edward, Jane's third brother who changed his surname to Knight when he inherited Godmersham.

Godmersham in June 1808, Jane wrote: 'The country is very beautiful. I saw as much as ever to admire in my yesterday's journey.' Jane set the fictional Pemberley in Derbyshire but she only had to only to raise her eyes and look out of her Godmersham window to see the type of landscape she was describing.

Visits to Kent by Jane and Cassandra, who were travelling from Bath or Hampshire, often lasted several months. The sisters were not usually there at the same time, so many of the surviving letters date from these visits. From these we learn that Jane saw the house in all its moods. Her first recorded visit in August 1798, accompanied by her parents and sister, was a quiet affair. The last took place in 1813 when the house was full of people, confusion and movement. Her letter of 15 June 1808 gives us a feel for the spacious interior:

'Our two brothers [Edward and James] were walking before the house as we approached, as natural as life. Fanny and Lizzy [two of Edward's children] met us in the Hall with a great deal of pleasant joy; we went for a few minutes into the breakfast parlour, and then proceeded to our rooms. Mary [James' Austen's wife] has the Hall chamber. I am in the Yellow room – very literally – for I am writing in it at this moment.

Godmersham was built around 1732 by Thomas Knight I. The wings were added in the 1770s; one for the kitchens, the other for the great library.

It seems odd to me to have such a great place all to myself, and to be at Godmersham without you is also odd'.

In one letter Jane says: 'In this house there is a constant succession of small events, somebody is always going or coming.' In another, when she finds herself in the great library she says: 'I am all alone. Edward is gone into his woods. At this present time I have five tables, eight-and-twenty chairs, and two fires all to myself.'

At Godmersham Jane was never really alone because in the same letter we hear: 'I did not mean to eat, but Mr. Johncock [the butler] has brought in the tray, so I must.' Mr Johncock would have been one of at least two dozen servants present in the house at any one time. During her visits Jane could enjoy for a short while the 'Elegance & Ease & luxury' where French wine was served instead of the usual home-made variety produced from Hampshire fruit.

On returning home to Hampshire in December 1798 Jane complained in a letter to Cassandra: 'People get so horridly poor & economical in this part of the World, that I have

Jane set the fictional Pemberley in Derbyshire but she only had to raise her eyes and look out of her Godmersham window to see the type of landscape she was describing.

Since 2001 Godmersham has been home to the college of The Association of British Dispensing Opticians (ABDO). (Photograph courtesy of Rebecca E. Lilley BA Hons)

The entrance hall at Godmersham.
(Photograph courtesy of Rebecca E. Lilley BA Hons)

*Much of the ornate interior plasterwork
remains that Jane would have known.*
(Photograph courtesy of Rebecca E. Lilley BA Hons)

no patience with them. Kent is the only place for happiness.'

On the other hand, it was in Kent she encountered the peculiarly rude, silent stare of the well-bred and the boring conversation of people whose pretensions exceeded their intelligence. At Godmersham Jane could be 'above Vulgar Economy' but before long she was ready to go home to 'the pleasure of friendship, of unreserved Conversation, of similarity of Taste & Opinions'.

Life at Godmersham followed a pattern, with visiting neighbours or receiving visits the main activity. When at home the men spent most of their time out of doors hunting, ferreting, shooting rabbits and game birds and fishing in the Stour for pike and eels. In the summer there were cricket matches and organised trips to the seaside. The ladies embroidered and sewed or walked in the park and garden. Jane in particular was always

Godmersham lies fairly low in the beautiful broad valley of the River Stour where the Austen men fished for pike and eels.

very involved with entertaining the children.

The social life of the house centred round dinner at the fashionable hour of six. Evenings were usually spent in conversation, playing cards, listening to either readings from a notable book or to a family member playing the harp or piano. Jane took the current manuscript she was working on with her. Marianne Knight, one of her nieces, recalled in old age:

'I remember that when Aunt Jane came to us at Godmersham she used to bring the manuscript of whatever novel she was writing with her, and would shut herself up with my elder sisters in one of the bedrooms to read them aloud. I and the younger ones used to hear peals of laughter through the door, and thought it very hard that we should be shut out from what was so delightful…I also remember how Aunt Jane would sit quietly working (at needlework) beside the fire in the library, saying nothing for a good while, and then would suddenly burst out laughing, jump up and run across the room to a table where pens and paper were lying, write something down, and then come back across to the fire and go on quietly working as before.'

Jane often mentions 'Sackree', the Godmersham children's nurse and family favourite.

In her letters Jane often mentions 'Sackree', the nursemaid at Godmersham from 1793 until her death in her ninetieth year, in 1851. She is referred to almost as a family member. When leaving Godmersham after her visit of 1805, Jane refers to her own poor relation status. She tells Cassandra she was charged only two shillings and sixpence by the travelling hairdresser where the other ladies paid five shillings. She also confides her financial state to her sister: 'As I find, on looking into my affairs, that instead of being very rich I am likely to be very poor, I cannot afford more than ten shillings for Sackree.'

Susan Sackree cared for many of the children of her original charges. A tribute in St Lawrence the Martyr church describes her as: 'The faithful servant and friend, for nearly sixty years, of Edward Knight, of Godmersham Park, and the beloved nurse of his children.'

Jane and the Godmersham family worshipped in the little village church where there is a memorial to Thomas and Catherine Knight. Cassandra was frequently invited to Godmersham to help Elizabeth with her confinements and, over the years, spent more time there than Jane. Elizabeth Knight was only thirty-five in 1808 when she died after giving birth to her eleventh child. She and Edward are commemorated on a large memorial in the nave and in a stained glass window in the chancel.

St Lawrence the Martyr church at Godmersham where Jane and her family worshipped.

12. Chilham and Chartham

CHILHAM

Jane Austen's letters are rich in references to Chilham and the Wildman family who owned the estate at the time. Jane and Cassandra were frequent visitors from nearby Godmersham attending dinners and balls at the castle. During the second week of January 1801, when Cassandra was staying at Godmersham, Jane wrote to her from Steventon: 'I am glad that the Wildmans are going to give a ball, and hope you will not fail to benefit both yourself and me by laying out a few kisses in the purchase of a frank,' which is another reference to Jane trying to curry favour with an MP in order to benefit from their privilege of free postage.

The following week she was commenting on Cassandra's experience: 'Your letter to Mary was duly received before she left Dean with Martha yesterday morning, and it gives us great pleasure to know that the Chilham ball was so agreeable, and that you danced four dances with Mr. Kemble. Desirable, however, as the latter circumstance was, I cannot

The picturesque village of Chilham is often used as a location for filming period dramas. In 2009 it was transformed into eighteenth-century Highbury *for the BBC's adaptation of Jane Austen's novel* Emma.

Chilham Castle, home to the Wildman family where Jane and Cassandra were guests at dinners and dances.

help wondering at its taking place. Why did you dance four dances with so stupid a man? Why not rather dance two of them with some elegant brother officer who was struck with your appearance as soon as you entered the room?'

The last letter we have of Jane's written at Godmersham begins by describing a dinner party at Chilham Castle on 6 November 1813:

'We met only the Bretons at Chilham Castle, besides a Mr. and Mrs. Osborne and a Miss Lee staying in the house, and were only fourteen altogether. My brother and Fanny thought it the pleasantest party they had ever known there, and I was very well entertained by bits and scraps. I had long wanted to see Dr. Breton, and his wife amuses me very much with her affected refinement and elegance. Miss Lee I found very conversable; she admires Crabbe as she ought. She is at an age of reason, ten years older than myself at least. She was at the famous ball at Chilham Castle, so of course you remember her. By the by, as I must leave off being young, I find many douceurs in being a sort of chaperon, for I am put on the sofa near the fire, and can drink as much wine as I like. We had music in the evening: Fanny and Miss Wildman played, and Mr. James Wildman sat close by and listened, or pretended to listen.'

The gardens and surrounding 300 acres of parkland are open to the public under the National Gardens Scheme.

When Jane talks of 'the famous ball at Chilham Castle', it seems she is referring to the ball that Cassandra attended twelve years earlier in 1801. The allusion conjures pictures of carriages, elegant gowns, dashing young officers and glittering chandeliers. The castle is now the private home of photographer and horsewoman Tessa Wheeler and her husband Stuart. In 2013 Tessa was behind a series of fund-raising events at Chilham Castle which included a sell-out commemorative Jane Austen Regency Ball.

In 1794, the Chilham estate was bought by Lancastrian James Wildman, who had prospered in Jamaica as agent for the fabulously wealthy William Beckford of Fonthill in Wiltshire. Wildman acquired some land from Beckford and a loan to build a sugar factory. He married Joanna Harper from Kingston in Jamaica, and within twelve years had become wealthy enough to buy the Chilham estate which included the village. We owe a particular debt to James Wildman for building the by-pass which has helped preserve Chilham as the showpiece we enjoy today.

The castle is now the private home of photographer and horsewoman Tessa Wheeler and her husband Stuart.

In 1816, when he was twenty-eight, James's son, James Beckford Wildman, inherited Chilham from his father. At the time the estate was worth £20,000 a year. Jane's niece Fanny, was twenty-three and she began to consider him as a potential future husband. Fanny was only fifteen when her mother died and from that time she seems to have looked to her aunt Jane for wisdom and advice especially in the area of love and courtship. On this occasion Jane wrote:

'My Dearest Fanny, You are inimitable, irresistible. You are the delight of my life. Such letters, such entertaining letters as you have lately sent! Such a description of your dear little heart! Such a lovely display of what Imagination does. You are worth your weight in Gold or even in the new Silver Coinage ... Oh! what a loss it will be when you are married. You are too agreeable in your single state, too agreeable as a Niece. I shall hate you when your delicious play of Mind is all settled down into conjugal and maternal affections. Mr J.W. frightens me. He will have you: I see you at the Altar... He must be wishing to attach you. It would be too stupid and too shameful in him to be otherwise; and all the Family are seeking your acquaintance. Do not imagine that I have any real objection. I have rather taken a fancy to him than not, and I like Chilham Castle for you; I only do not like you should marry anybody. And yet I do wish you to marry very much, because I know you will never be happy till you are; but the loss of a Fanny Knight will be never made up to me; My "Affectionate Niece F. G. Wildman" will be but a poor Substitute.'

The fine Wildman Memorial in the church was commissioned in memory of James Wildman by his grieving family. The monument is by Sir Francis Chantrey, the most famous English sculptor of his time who was responsible for several great statues in the capital. It is a measure of the Wildman wealth and aspirations that they were able to employ Sir Francis.

Through his friendship with William Wilberforce, James Beckford Wildman was persuaded to the abolition cause. He planned to purchase machinery to work the sugar plantations and set his slaves free. The cost of this together with his over generous provisions for members of his family meant that in 1861 Chilham had to be sold.

The moving Wildman Memorial in St Mary's church is by famous sculptor Sir Francis Chantrey.

Chilham Rectory home to the Tyldens in Jane's time.
(Photograph courtesy of Tony Stables)

79

CHARTHAM

Mystole House at Chartham, is located on the Great Stour River in the vale of the Kent Downs in an Area of Outstanding Natural Beauty. In Jane's time the house was home to Rev'd Sir John Fagg and his daughters with whom Jane visited with little pleasure.

In 1806, when she was thirteen, Jane's niece Fanny wrote to her former governess Dorothy Chapman: 'I think I quite agree with you, as to miss Fagg's plainness, poor thing! To be sure she is unfortunately ugly.'

On 12 October 1813 Jane was anticipating a visit to Mystole: 'Disastrous Letters from the Plumptres & Oxendens. - Refusals everywhere - a Blank partout - & it is not quite certain whether we go or not; - something may depend upon the disposition of Uncle Edward when he comes - & upon what we hear at Chilham Castle this morng - for we are

The Great Stour at Chartham.

The splendid sixteenth-century mansion of Mystole is now divided into private apartments.

going to pay visits. We are going to each house at Chilham & to Mystole. I shall like seeing the Faggs. - I shall like it all, except that we are to set out so early that I have not time to write as I could wish.'

When Jane speaks of 'each house at Chilham' she is referring to the castle and the Rectory, home of the Tyldens. On the 14 October she gives Cassandra a report of her visit to Mystole:

'I was surprised to find Mystole so pretty. The ladies were at home. I was in luck, and saw Lady Fagg and all her five daughters, with an old Mrs. Hamilton, from Canterbury, and Mrs. and Miss Chapman, from Margate, into the bargain. I never saw so plain a family — five sisters so very plain! They are as plain as the Foresters, or the Franfraddops, or the Seagraves, or the Rivers, excluding Sophy. Miss Sally Fagg has a pretty figure, and that comprises all the good looks of the family.'

'It was stupidish; Fanny did her part very well, but there was a lack of talk altogether, and the three friends in the house only sat by and looked at us. However, Miss Chapman's name is Laura, and she had a double flounce to her gown. You really must get some flounces. Are not some of your large stock of white morning gowns just in a happy state for a flounce – too short? Nobody at home at either house in Chilham.'

The splendid mansion of Mystole House stands in the south-west corner of the parish and is now divided into private apartments. It was built in the sixteenth-century by John Bungay, Rector of Chartham, and later became the seat of the Fagg family whose fine historic monument can be seen in St Mary's church.

13. Canterbury

In her letter of 23 January 1799 Jane expressed a desire to travel to Deal with her brother Charles who was joining his ship, the *Tamar*: 'I want to go with him, that I may explain the country to him properly between Canterbury and Rowling.' It was through visits to her brother Edward and his family at Rowling that Jane first became familiar with Canterbury when she was still in her teens.

The main attractions were plays and concerts at the theatre, balls held at the assembly rooms, and the haberdashery shops. At a concert one night Jane observed that: 'the races of Bridges and Plumptre seem to have come in force from Goodnestone and Fredville, and to have had a pleasant time of it.' On another she tells Cassandra: 'I am without silk. You must get me some in town or in Canterbury.' [The Bridges spelt with an 'i' are from Goodnestone, the Brydges spelt with a 'y' are from Wooton Court.]

Balls were held monthly through the winter at Delmar's Assembly Rooms above the Canterbury Bank. On 1 December 1800 Jane says to Cassandra: 'Pray do not forget to go to the Canterbury Ball. I shall despise you all most insufferably if you do.- By the bye, there will not be any Ball, because Delmar lost so much by the Assemblies last winter that he has protested against opening his rooms this year.' Delmar's Rooms were above a bank on a corner facing the High Street. The present day building on the site is still used as a bank.

Thomas Knight II died in 1794 and three years later, his widow Catherine turned over control of the Godmersham estate to Edward. Mrs Knight retained an income of £2,000 for herself and moved to a town house called White Friars in Canterbury. In letters written after this time we hear of Jane sometimes spending a few days at Goodnestone with the Bridges family, and sometimes visiting and sleeping over at White Friars.

The mansion was located on the site of a former monastic complex occupied by the Austin friars or 'White Friars', whose twelfth-century monastery had been dissolved by Henry VIII in 1538. It was converted into a house with fine gardens and orchards in the sixteenth-century. Visiting White Friars and Mrs Knight's Canterbury circle of friends added a new dimension to Jane's social sphere. A typical commentary on events was given to Cassandra in a letter dated Sunday 26 June 1808:

'Mr. Knatchbull, from Provender, was at the W. Friars when we arrived, and stayed dinner, which, with Harriot, who came, as you may suppose, in a great hurry, ten minutes after the time, made our number six. Mr. K. went away early; Mr. Moore

Canterbury Cathedral, so familiar to Jane, where for centuries pilgrims made their way to the shrine of the martyr Saint Thomas Becket.

Clockwise from top left: *Mrs Brydges rented 11 The Precincts. Now called Cathedral House, it is the offices and registered address of the Dean and Chapter of Canterbury; The Oaks, an area on the east side of the Cathedral precincts, where Mrs Moore, the Archbishop's widow lived; Reverend Thomas Powys lived at The Deanery which adjoins Marlowe House and dominates on the east side of Green Court; 17 The Precincts, Linacre House, was home to Archdeacon Reverend Dr John Lynch, and his family with whom Jane dined.*

Mrs Charles Milles lived for a time here at Meister Omer's House; she later moved to 9 The Precincts and finally to 14C.

The Great Stour adds attraction to the Canterbury scene as it flows under the High Street.

succeeded him, and we sat quietly working and talking till 10, when he ordered his wife away, and we adjourned to the dressing-room to eat our tart and jelly… Mrs. C. Knatchbull and I breakfasted *tête-à-tête* the next day, for her husband was gone to Mr. Toke's, and Mrs. Knight had a sad headache which kept her in bed. She had had too much company the day before.

After my coming, which was not till past two, she had Mrs. Milles, of Nackington, a Mrs. and Miss Gregory, and Charles Graham; and she told me it had been so all the morning. Very soon after breakfast on Friday, Mrs. C. K., who is just what we have always seen her, went with me to Mrs. Brydges, and Mrs. Moore's, paid some other visits while I remained with the latter, and we finished with Mrs. C. Milles, who luckily was not at home, and whose new house is a very convenient short cut from the Oaks to the W. Friars.'

Above left: *Mediaeval streets where Jane shopped still survive around the area of the Cathedral.*

Above right: *Delmar's Assembly Rooms, which Jane mentions, were over a former bank that stood on this High Street site.*

Through Catherine Knight's introductions Jane became very familiar with the Cathedral precincts and its residents. Although the city was heavily bombed during the Second World War most of the houses Jane visited survive. Mrs Moore, the Archbishop's widow, lived in an area on the east side of the precincts called The Oaks. The present Dean and Chapter of Canterbury have their offices in a property now known as Cathedral House. In Jane's time this was a private house simply known as number 11 and rented by Mrs Brydges.

The Reverend Thomas Powys lived in the Deanery which adjoins Marlowe House and dominates the east side of Green Court. Mrs Charles Milles and her daughter 'Molly' or 'Moy' lived for fifty years at Meister Omer's House. The garrulous Molly and her aged mother could well have been inspirations for Miss Bates and her mother in *Emma*.

On 26 October 1813 Jane told Cassandra: 'Miss Milles was queer as usual, and provided us with plenty to laugh at. She undertook in three words to give us the history of Mrs. Scudamore's reconciliation, and then talked on about it for half-an-hour, using such odd expressions, and so foolishly minute, that I could hardly keep my countenance.'

Canterbury Gaol in Longport where Jane visited in November 1813 is no longer a prison. It is now used as accommodation for students of Canterbury Christ Church University.

One dramatic change of routine occurred on 3 November 1813 when Edward, in his role as a magistrate, visited Canterbury Gaol in Longport and Jane accompanied him. She reported: 'Edward & I had a delightful morning for our drive there, I enjoyed it thoroughly, but the Day turned off before we were ready, & we came home in some rain & the apprehension of a great deal. It has not done us any harm, however. – He went to inspect the Gaol, as a visiting Magistrate, & took me with him. – I was gratified – & went through all the feelings which People must go through, I think in visiting such a building.' However, the next sentence is quintessential Austen: 'We paid no other visits only walked about snugly together & shopp'd – I bought a Concert Ticket & a sprig of flowers for my old age.'

14. Ashford, Godinton and Mersham

ASHFORD

Several times in her letters from Godmersham Jane mentions Assembly Balls held at Ashford, but never with much enthusiasm. In 1798 she referred to having attended a ball there in September which she had not much enjoyed due to the crowded room and hot weather. Fifteen years later, on the 14 October 1813, she was at breakfast with Fanny then aged twenty and they were discussing the idea of attending a ball that evening but decide against it:

'We did not go to the ball. It was left to her to decide, and at last she determined against it. She knew that it would be a sacrifice on the part of her father and brothers if they went, and I hope it will prove that *she* has not sacrificed much. It is not likely that there should have been anybody there whom she would care for. *I* was very glad to be spared the trouble of dressing and going, and being weary before it was half over, so my gown and my cap are still unworn. It will appear at last, perhaps, that I might have done without either. I produced my brown bombazine yesterday, and it was very much admired indeed, and I like it better than ever.'

The dances were held in rooms above an inn at 56 High Street, Ashford known as the 'Saracens Head Family & Commercial Hotel & Posting House'. An advertisement from

A modern Boots store now occupies the site of the Saracen's Head Inn where Jane attended balls in the assembly room.

Jane would have known the centuries-old George Inn which is a few steps from the site of the assembly room.

the *Kentish Gazette or Canterbury Chronicle* of September 1768 reads: 'Price 2d. On Thursday next, the 20th Inst. there will be a Card and Dancing Assembly at the "Saracen Head" at Ashford'. A modern branch of Boots Chemist now occupies the site.

A few doors along on the same side is a building Jane would have known. The George Inn is mentioned in a will of 1533 and the building has been an inn for four centuries. It originally had an inn sign which stretched across the width of the High Street.

GODINTON PARK

Godinton House is a stately home in the parish of Great Chart, 2 miles north-west of the centre of Ashford. The house was for centuries the home of the Toke family who are mentioned from time to time in Jane's letters. She attended social functions in Canterbury and Nackington and met members of the Toke family whom she had probably met previously at Godmersham and Goodnestone. The Knights would have visited Godinton, and it is very likely that Jane accompanied them although there is no direct reference to this in her correspondence.

During Jane's time, the head of the family was Mr John Toke (1738-1819), a contemporary of her father. Mr Toke was a distinguished member of the local gentry and served for a time as High Sheriff of Kent – a post which Jane's brother Edward held later.

Godinton House near Ashford was the seat of the Toke family for about 455 years from 1440 to 1895.

The 'Great' Chamber at Godinton is actually one of a succession of intimate rooms gleaming with carved and polished oak.

Writing to Cassandra from Godmersham on 16 October 1813 Jane said: 'Mr. Toke I am always very fond of. He inquired after you and my mother, which adds esteem to passion.'

Earlier in 1796, Jane reported to Cassandra that John Toke senior and his second son (also named John) were with a party at Nackington House: 'I took an opportunity of assuring Mr. J. T. that neither he nor his father need longer keep themselves single for you.' It proved to be rather prophetic. Jane was referring to the fact that a year earlier Cassandra had become engaged to Reverend Thomas Fowle. In February 1797, when Tom Fowle was part of an expedition to the West Indies he caught yellow fever and died.

In 1762, John Toke senior had married Margaret Roundell and their eldest son Nicholas Roundell Toke, who was nearly ten years older than Jane, became a favourite of hers. Many of the county set she socialised with were aloof but Nicholas was sympathetic. The main preoccupation of the majority of the men she encountered in East Kent was hunting. Nicholas Toke was different. He was the most scholarly member of the family, a

Above left: *John Toke married Margaret Roundell in 1762 and eight years later he became High Sheriff of Kent. This portrait shows him in the robes of office.*

Above right: *The carved staircase is one of the wonders of Godinton and was created for Captain Nicholas Toke in 1628.*

translator of Greek inscriptions and a correspondent with leading antiquaries. In a letter to Cassandra on 20 November 1800 Jane said: 'there are few people whom I like better'.

John Toke junior was born in 1766, and in due course was ordained and became Vicar of Bekesbourne and Rector of Harbledown. The daughter of the family, Mary, married Edward Scudamore in 1813 – a physician, surgeon and apothecary who makes an occasional appearance in Jane's letters attending the Knights.

The carved staircase is one of the wonders of Godinton and was created for Captain Nicholas Toke in 1628. Did Jane have this staircase (or perhaps its rival at Knole) in mind when General Tilney gives Catherine Morland a tour of Northanger Abbey?: 'They returned to the hall, that the chief staircase might be ascended, and the beauty of its wood, and ornaments of rich carving might be pointed out: having gained the top, they turned in an opposite direction from the gallery in which her room lay.'

Writing of the interior and the magnificent staircase in particular, Nigel Nicholson in *The World of Jane Austen* says: 'Did Jane ever see it? She never specifically says she did, but I need little persuading that my hand is resting where hers rested too.'

In 1991 Major Alan Wyndham-Green, the last owner of Godinton, established the Godinton House Preservation Trust. Since his passing in 1996 the Trust has continued to preserve, restore, and enhance the house and parklands.

Godinton today is a comfortable, much-loved home; each room has a different feel, a contrast on a theme, not designed by architect or curator but for the taste and enjoyment of those who lived here over the centuries. It is open for visitors on summer afternoons from Friday to Sunday and on Bank Holiday Mondays. On each day tours of the house are led by expert guides. The gardens are open from March to November.

*Godinton is an imposing
Stuart mansion surrounded
by its own parkland.*

MERSHAM LE HATCH

The estate of Mersham le Hatch had been in the hands of the Knatchbull family for nearly three hundred years before Jane Austen was born. It was the childhood home of Catherine Knight née Knatchbull who adopted Jane's brother Edward.

There is no certainty that Jane ever visited the house but her familiar abbreviation 'Hatch' suggests that she might have known it quite well. If she did see it, Mersham would have been the only Robert Adam-designed house she knew. Three years after Jane's death Mersham le Hatch became the home of Fanny Knight after her marriage in 1820 to Sir Edward Knatchbull.

Today the house and park are strictly private but the outbuildings in the cobbled coach yard have been converted into shops and the coach house is now a restaurant.

Mersham le Hatch is the only Robert Adam-designed house Jane would have known.

The coach house at Mersham is now a restaurant.

The cobbled coaching yard is accessible to the public but the house and park are strictly private.

15. Eastwell Park

Bordering Godmersham to the south-west is the even larger estate of Eastwell Park. This was the seat of the Hatton family for over 250 years until 1893. In Jane Austen's time the Knights and Hattons met regularly in each other's homes and also socialised with other families from the great houses of East Kent.

In expectation of an inheritance, George Finch (1747-1823) added Hatton to his name in 1764. In 1785 he married Lady Elizabeth Murray and they had five children. In later life their eldest son, also named George, famously fought a duel with the Duke of Wellington when the latter was Prime Minister. The youngest son Daniel, who was a favourite of Jane Austen's, later became Chaplain to Queen Victoria.

George's unmarried sisters, the Misses Anne and Mary Finch did not add Hatton to their name. The third sister Harriet, married Sir Jenison-William Gordon in 1781. Jane often mentions the Hatton family in her correspondence. The first reference is in a letter to Cassandra written from Godmersham on Saturday 24 August 1805 in which she says: 'Our visit to Eastwell was very agreeable; I found Ly. Gordon's manners as pleasing as they had been described, and saw nothing to dislike in Sir Janison, excepting once or twice a sort of sneer at Mrs. Anne Finch. He was just getting into talk with Elizabeth as the carriage was ordered, but during the first part of the visit he said very little.'

Today Eastwell serves as a sumptuous country house hotel and is a perfect base for exploring the Jane Austen locations of East Kent.

The present day Eastwell Manor was re-built in 1926 as a replica of an actual Elizabethan mansion.

Although Jane would not recognise the present house, she was obviously very familiar with the surrounding landscape and would have walked in the gardens and played here on the lawns with the Finch-Hatton children.

Jane also comments: 'They were very civil to me, as they always are', which implies earlier visits and goes on to report: '…fortune was also very civil to me in placing Mr. E. Hatton by me at dinner. I have discovered that Lady Elizabeth, for a woman of her age and situation, has astonishingly little to say for herself, and that Miss Hatton has not much more. Her eloquence lies in her fingers; they were most fluently harmonious.' Although Jane found the women of the family cool and standoffish she was very taken with the children: 'George is a fine boy, and well behaved, but Daniel chiefly delighted me; the good humour of his countenance is quite bewitching. After tea we had a cribbage-table, and he and I won two rubbers off his brother and Mrs. Mary.'

Writing on Friday 30 June 1808 Jane describes a visit by the Finch-Hattons to Godmersham: 'Lady E. Hatton called here a few mornings ago, her Daughter Elizabeth with her, who says as little as ever, but holds up her head & smiles & is to be at the Races.' In a similar account a month later Jane says: 'they came, they sat and they went'. Perhaps the silent Elizabeth has her counterpart in the silent Anne de Bourgh in *Pride and Prejudice*?

By the end of the summer things had not improved. On Tuesday 26 October we hear that: 'George Hatton called yesterday, and I saw him, saw him for ten minutes; sat in the same room with him, heard him talk, saw him bow, and was not in raptures. I discerned nothing extraordinary. I should speak of him as a gentlemanlike young man – *eh! bien tout est dit*. We are expecting the ladies of the family this morning.'

The Eastwell that Jane knew was designed by Joseph Bonomi, the architect she mentions in Sense and Sensibility.

A couple of years later, Fanny Knight was causing hearts to flutter in the neighbourhood. At seventeen she was first interested in the nineteen-year-old George William Finch-Hatton and she used an astronomical code in her diary to describe him, calling him 'Jupiter' or 'the Planet'. Cassandra repressed this infatuation. Three years later, in 1813, Jane reports on the comings and goings of the two families:

'We hear a great deal of George Hatton's wretchedness. I suppose he has quick feelings – but I dare say they will not kill him. – He is so much out of spirits however that his friend John Plumptre (of Fredville Park, Nonnington) is gone over to comfort him, at Mr Hatton's desire; he called here this morning in his way. A handsome young Man certainly, with quiet, gentlemanlike manners. – I set him down as sensible rather than Brilliant. – There is nobody Brilliant nowadays. – He talks of staying a week at Eastwell & then comes to Chilham Castle: for a day or two, & my Brother invited him to come here afterwards, which he seemed very agreable to.'

Fanny confirms in a letter that: 'all the young ladies were in love with George Hatton – he was very handsome and agreeable, danced very well, and flirted famously.' Jane's young niece's interest turned next to John Plumptre and then to James Wildman of Chilham Castle. George Hatton recovered from his melancholia and soon after married Lady Charlotte Graham whom Fanny called 'a sweet little perfection'.

The Eastwell Park mansion that Jane knew has a special significance because, like Laverstoke in Hampshire, it was a new house designed by the Italian immigrant Joseph Bonomi, the only architect whom Jane refers to by name in her novels- though not favourably. It was the third house on its site and the style was alien to the English tradition and defied the English classical rules by having an immense arched portico. Perhaps it was this ostentation that elicited Jane's poor opinion of Bonomi.

In *Sense and Sensibility* it was Bonomi who was responsible for the country house plans that the insufferable Robert Ferrars flung on to the fire. The present day Eastwell Manor was re-built in 1926 as a replica of an actual Elizabethan mansion, Cell Park, Markyate in Hertfordshire. Today it serves as a sumptuous country house hotel and is a perfect base for exploring the Jane Austen locations of East Kent.

Although Jane would not recognise the present house she was obviously very familiar with the surrounding landscape and would have walked in the gardens and played on the lawns with the Finch-Hatton children.

Eastwell Manor today is furnished in a classical style yet has all the modern facilities you would expect from a first class family-run country house hotel.

16. Lenham

The twelfth-century church of St Mary at Lenham where Edward was vicar during Jane Austen's time.

Opposite: *The Vicarage at Lenham seen from the churchyard was home to Rev'd Edward Bridges.*

There continue to be new biographies of Jane Austen and innumerable prequels and sequels to her novels. Screen writer Gwyneth Hughes went a step further with her 2007 film *Miss Austen Regrets*. Perhaps taking heart from Mark Twain's famous quote: 'Never let the truth stand in the way of a good story,' she speculated on events that took place in East Kent.

The story weaves together Edward Bridges' flirtation with Jane and his proposal of marriage; Jane's early infatuation with Rev'd Edward Taylor of Patrixbourne and Fanny Knight's adolescent love for John Pemberton Plumptre of Fredville.

Using Jane's own words where possible the film presents us with a portrait of Edward Bridges as a sadly regretted suitor. In this case, as with much of Jane's life, the truth is elusive because the letters which would have given us an accurate insight were burned by Cassandra. Nevertheless people do continue to find it entertaining to speculate as to 'what might have been'.

Reverend Brook Edward Bridges (known as Edward) was four years younger than Jane. He was one of thirteen children born to Sir Brook William Bridges, third baronet of Goodnestone and his wife Fanny Fowler. All the Bridges sons were named Brook (Brook William, Brook Henry, Brook Edward, Brook George, etc). With so many younger sons in one family, it is not surprising that many of them looked to the church for their profession. As a clergyman, Edward Bridges had lifetime holdings in Kent at Wingham and at Lenham, where he resided in the vicarage.

We have already seen in the chapter on Rowling, Jane proudly telling her sister that at Goodnestone in 1796 she: '...opened the ball with Edward Bridges'. And in 1805 we learned it was impossible to do justice to the hospitality of Edward's attentions towards her when he made a point of ordering toasted cheese for supper entirely on her account.

It was three years after this event that Edward made his proposal which Jane seems to have checked or dismissed lightly. On 7 October 1808 she wrote to Cassandra: 'I wish you may be able to accept Lady Bridges's invitation, though *I* could not her son Edward's; she is a nice Woman, & honours me by her remembrance.'

A month later Jane received the news that Edward had become engaged to Harriet Foote, his sister-in-law. Her reaction showed no regret: 'Your news of Edw: Bridges was quite news... I wish him happy with all my heart, & hope his choice may turn out

The Dog & Bear and the Red Lion coaching inns grace one side of Lenham's picturesque market square.

according to his own expectations, & beyond those of his Family – And I dare say it will. Marriage is a great Improver – & in a similar situation Harriet may be as amiable as Eleanor [Harriet's sister, first wife of Brook William Bridges]. – As to Money, that will come You may be sure, because they cannot do without it. – When you see him again, pray give him our Congratulations & best wishes.' The letter ends rather cryptically: 'Martha [Lloyd] sends her best Love, & thanks you for admitting her to the knowledge of the pros and cons about Harriet Foote.'

In 1809, Edward and Harriet married and went on to have several children. Jane's references to the couple after this time are comments on the frequent journeys Edward made between Lenham and Ramsgate where his wife lodged due to her weak constitution and need for sea air. On 25 October 1813 she wrote from Godmersham: 'In this house there is a constant succession of small events, somebody is always coming or going.; this morng we had Edwd Bridges unexpectedly to breakfast with us, in his way from Ramsgate where is his wife, to Lenham where is his Church – & tomorrow he dines and sleeps here on his return. – They have been all summer at Ramsgate, for her health, she is a poor Honey – the sort of woman who gives me the idea of being determined never to be well – & who likes her spasms & nervousness & the consequence they give her better than anything else'. A condition echoed in the characters of Mary Musgrove in *Persuasion* and Susan Parker in *Sanditon*.

Edward used to break his journey by staying at Goodnestone or Godmersham. He sometimes had a friend with him and Jane began to suspect him of taking advantage of her brother's generosity. On 14 October 1813 she wrote: 'Edward Bridges and his friend did not forget to arrive. The friend is a Mr. Wigram, one of the three-and-twenty children of a great rich mercantile, Sir Robert Wigram, an old acquaintance of the Footes, but very recently known to Edward B. The history of his coming here is, that, intending to go from Ramsgate to Brighton, Edw. B. persuaded him to take Lenham on his way, which gave him the convenience of Mr. W.'s gig, and the comfort of not being alone there; but, probably thinking a few days of Gm. would be the cheapest and pleasantest way of entertaining his friend and himself, offered a visit here, and here they stay till to-morrow.'

Fanny Knight (Imogen Poots), Jane Austen (Olivia Williams) and Cassandra (Greta Scacchi) in Gwyneth Hughes's imaginative film Miss Austen Regrets.

In the end she began to feel sorry for him and in a letter of 26 October 1813 she said: 'We have had another of Edward Bridges' Sunday visits. I think the pleasantest part of his married life must be the dinners, and breakfasts, and luncheons, and billiards that he gets in this way at Gm. Poor wretch! he is quite the dregs of the family as to luck.'

1813 was the last year of Jane's visits to Godmersham. In a letter of 7 November she told Cassandra about her plans to stay at their brother Henry's London house in Henrietta Street on her way home to Hampshire: 'We are to be off on Saturday before the post comes in, as Edward takes his own horses all the way. He talks of 9 o'clock. We shall bait at Lenham.' (To 'bait' meant to stop for rest and refreshment both for travellers and their horses).

Lenham is a pretty market village on the southern edge of the North Downs, halfway between Maidstone and Ashford. The picturesque square retains two coaching inns; The Red Lion and the Dog & Bear. Lenham's vicarage is now divided into flats, but it's easy to imagine what it must have been like when Jane Austen was here in November 1813. Rev'd Edward Bridges died in Wingham in 1825, his 'invalid' wife Harriet outlived him by nearly forty years, dying in 1864.

17. Barham and Broome Park

By 1798 Jane had already enjoyed a couple of extended holidays in East Kent and had met members of the Oxenden family from Broome Park at Barham. Broome Park is just 6 miles south-east of Canterbury and less than 10 miles from Godmersham as the crow flies. However, it is another of those tantalising places that Jane could easily have visited but we will probably never know for certain if she did.

In a letter of 30 August 1805 Jane mentions Edward Bridges visiting Broome Park, which was owned at that time by Sir Henry Oxenden and his wife Mary Graham. Mary

Broome Park, one of the finest seventeenth-century houses in England, was home to Fanny Knight's friend Mary Oxenden.

Today Broome Park is a leisure development centre where you can buy a time share apartment with access to a country club.

Broome Park as it would have looked in the days when Fanny Knight visited Mary Oxenden.

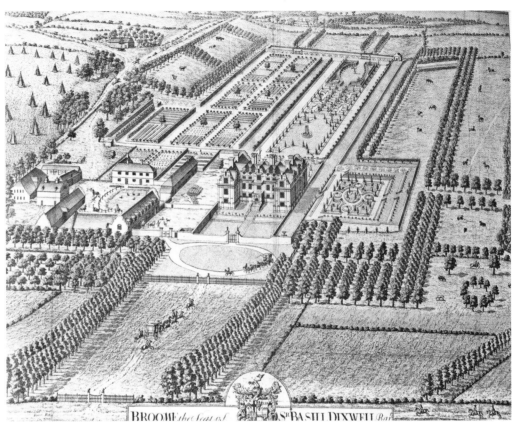

Below: : *Sir Henry Oxenden whom Jane reported was not very tenderly treated in Samuel Egerton Brydges novel* Fitz-Albini.

bore Henry twelve children of whom eleven survived him. Sir Henry's eldest daughter (also named Mary) became a friend of Fanny Knight and is mentioned in a number of Jane's letters, particularly in respect to attending balls and there is this cryptic comment in a letter of 24 August 1814: 'Mary Oxenden, instead of dieing, is going to marry Wm Hammond.'

Back in 1786, when Jane Austen was eleven, new neighbours arrived at Steventon in Hampshire where she was born and spent her early life. Samuel Egerton Brydges rented the parsonage at Deane from Jane's father George and moved in with his new wife Elizabeth and younger sister Charlotte. In her letters Jane refers to him as 'Egerton'.

Egerton had moved to Hampshire to be near his sister, Mrs Anne Lefroy née Brydges. Anne had married the Reverend Isaac Peter George Lefroy who became rector at Ashe. Both Egerton and Anne had been born at Wootton in Kent.

Anne, who became Jane's beloved friend and mentor was also an inspiration for her own younger brother Egerton. Unhappily, his literary talent was unequal to his ambition and disappointed at the muted response to his published poems, he moved back to Kent.

In December 1798 Jane wrote to Cassandra, who was staying at Godmersham, reporting her concerns about a novel Egerton had written which contained some thinly disguised portraits of his Kent neighbours:

'We have got Fitz-Albini; my father has bought it against my private wishes, for it does not quite satisfy my feelings that we should purchase the only one of Egerton's works of which his family are ashamed. That these scruples, however, do not at all interfere with my reading it, you will easily believe. We have neither of us yet finished the first volume. My father is disappointed – I am not, for I expected nothing better. Never did any book carry more internal evidence of its author. Every sentiment is

The estate was bought in 1911 by Lord Kitchener whose portrait hangs on the back wall in the great hall.

Sir Henry died on 22 September 1838 at Broome Park and was buried in Barham church which was draped in black. One of the ten pall bearers was his old friend the Duke of Wellington.

The Oxenden memorial in St John the Baptist church, Barham.

completely Egerton's. There is very little story, and what there is told in a strange, unconnected way. There are many characters introduced, apparently merely to be delineate. We have not been able to recognise any of them hitherto, except Dr. and Mrs. Hey and Mr. Oxenden, who is not very tenderly treated. . . .'

Egerton eventually turned to genealogical, antiquarian and bibliographical writing. He even financed his own printing press at Lee Priory, Ickham, publishing beautiful editions of other people's work.

Broome Park is one of the finest seventeenth-century houses in England. It was built between 1635 and 1638, half way through the golden age of brick building which flourished with Henry VII and Queen Anne. It passed to the Oxenden family in 1750. It is now a leisure development centre where you can buy a time share apartment with access to a country club.

18. Ramsgate

From the time of the Roman invasion in 55BC and the conquest of England by William the Norman in 1066 right up to the Second World War, the counties of Kent and Sussex have always been in the front line for threats of incursion by enemy forces.

Following the outbreak of the French Revolution and France's declaration of war on Great Britain in 1793, the defence of the English Channel and the south coast was given the highest priority. From that time, with the exception of a short breathing space provided by the Peace of Amiens in 1802/03, Jane Austen's naval brothers Francis and Charles were actively engaged in war at sea and the defence of the coast.

Napoleon had concentrated his Grand Army in the French Maritime Provinces where he ordered the Bayeux Tapestry to be paraded in public to arouse enthusiasm for his planned triumphant crossing of the Channel. The English Channel Fleet was ready to turn back the flat-bottomed barges in which Napoleon hoped to transport his troops and horses in favourable weather. On land, a Home Guard with the title of 'Sea Fencibles' was created as a second line of defence should the French succeed in landing on the Kent or Sussex beaches.

At the renewal of hostilities in 1803, Francis Austen was appointed to embody and command the North Foreland unit of Sea Fencibles whose headquarters were in Ramsgate. It was here where he met his future wife Mary Gibson. Francis was twenty-nine and Mary was just nineteen. She was a fair-haired, cheerful and practical young lady and Frank proposed to her soon after they met. They were officially engaged in 1804 and, like many young naval officers, Frank planned to marry as soon as he had gained sufficient prize money from successful actions against the enemy.

Jane's references to Ramsgate in both her letters and her novels are consistent with a knowledge of the town and a dislike of it. Mary Gibson was born in Ramsgate on 14 September 1784 and baptised the following May in St Laurence church, where her parents John Gibson and Mary Curling had married the previous year. On 21 August 1785 Mary's mother died, possibly as a result of a second pregnancy. She was aged twenty-six and her daughter was thirteen months. There is a monument on the south wall of the church to: 'Mary, the beloved wife of John Gibson of Ramsgate'.

When Francis Austen met the Gibson family they were living in a comfortable house in Ramsgate High Street and John Gibson was commanding a company of Ramsgate Loyal Volunteers. According to the Ramsgate Society, Francis lived for a while at 14

According to The Ramsgate Society, Francis Austen lived at 14 Albion Place where Jane visited him in 1803.

At the renewal of hostilities in 1803, Francis Austen was appointed to embody and command the North Foreland unit of Sea Fencibles.

Albion Place, and Jane visited him there in 1803. A decade later, when she came to write *Mansfield Park*, she had Tom Bertram's friends the Sneyds stay in Albion Place.

Francis remained in Ramsgate for ten months until May 1804, when he received a commission for the *Leopard*, a 50 gun ship-of-the-line. In August 1804 Jane's brother Edward rented 7 and 8 Sion Hill to accommodate his large family party for their summer holiday.

Jane confirms her dislike for Ramsgate in a letter to Cassandra written on 14 October 1813: 'Ed Hussey is warned out of Pet and talks of fixing at Ramsgate – Bad taste! He is very fond of the sea, however. Some taste in that, and some judgement, too, in fixing on Ramsgate, as being by the sea'. The Hussey family of Scotney Castle in Kent were known to the Austens and linked to them by marriage. Edward Hussey, a friend of Jane's brother Edward, rented Pet Place at Charing in Kent.

Jane used her experience of Ramsgate in two of her novels, *Pride and Prejudice*

In August 1804 Jane's brother Edward rented 7 and 8 Sion Hill to accommodate his large family party for their summer holiday. The houses, destroyed in the Second World War, stood on the site next to the Foy Boat Hotel.

The construction of Ramsgate Harbour began in 1749. Because of its proximity to mainland Europe, Ramsgate was a chief embarkation point both during the Napoleonic Wars and for the Dunkirk evacuation in 1940.

Albion Place can be seen in the centre background of this Georgian sketch with the Albion Hotel further to the right.

published in 1813 and *Mansfield Park* the following year. In *Pride and Prejudice*, fifteen-year-old Georgiana Darcy is taken to the town by her companion Mrs Younge and persuaded to elope with Mr Wickham, who has his eye on the teenager's fortune. In chapter thirty-five Mr Darcy explains the situation to Elizabeth Bennett:

'My sister, who is more than ten years my junior, was left to the guardianship of my mother's nephew, Colonel Fitzwilliam, and myself. About a year ago she was taken from school, and an establishment formed for her in London; and last summer she went with the lady who presided over it to Ramsgate; and thither also went Mr. Wickham, undoubtedly by design...'

In Chapter thirty-five Lady Catherine de Bourgh refers to the situation: 'When my niece Georgiana went to Ramsgate last summer, I made a point of her having two men-servants go with her. Miss Darcy, the daughter of Mr Darcy, of Pemberley, and Lady Anne, could not have appeared with propriety in a different manner. I am excessively attentive to all those things.'

In chapter forty-three Elizabeth Bennet visits Pemberley in the company of her aunt and uncle Mr and Mrs Gardiner and they are shown round by Mrs Reynolds the housekeeper. They were admiring a portrait of Mr Darcy when:

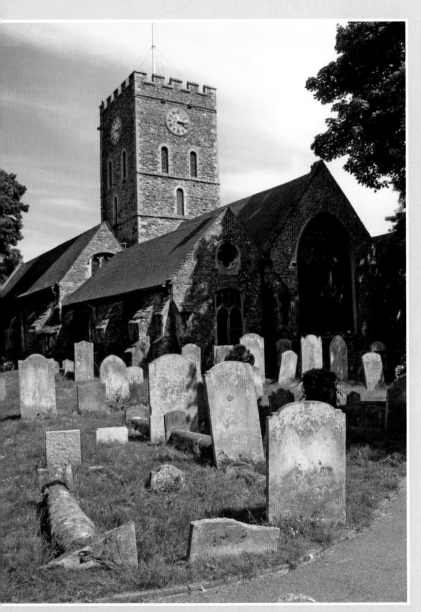

Above: *The daughter of a Victorian vicar painted this picture of the interior of St Laurence showing its original box pews and gallery. This and another of her paintings hang in the vestry.*

Left: *The monument on the south wall of the church to: 'Mary, the beloved wife of John Gibson of Ramsgate'.*

St Laurence church, Ramsgate where Francis Austen and Mary Gibson were married on 24 July 1806.

Above left: *Looking down Hardres Street towards the junction with High Street, the Gibson's 'comfortable house' is on the left just beyond the house with the two-storey bow windows. The imposing building in the background is George Sanger's Amphitheatre. Built in 1883 as a circus building it was later used for opera, drama and talking pictures before being demolished in 1960.*
(Courtesy of Terry Wheeler, Ramsgate Historical Society)

Above right: *The Gibson's house at No. 51 High Street was demolished and replaced by a bank. It is now a branch of F. Hinds the jewellers.*

'Mrs. Reynolds then directed their attention to one of Miss Darcy, drawn when she was only eight years old. "And is Miss Darcy as handsome as her brother?" said Mr. Gardiner. "Oh! yes – the handsomest young lady that ever was seen; and so accomplished! – She plays and sings all day long. In the next room is a new instrument just come down for her – a present from my master; she comes here to-morrow with him." Mr. Gardiner, whose manners were easy and pleasant, encouraged her communicativeness by his questions and remarks; Mrs. Reynolds, either from pride or attachment, had evidently great pleasure in talking of her master and his sister.'

"Is your master much at Pemberley in the course of the year?" "Not so much as I could wish, Sir; but I dare say he may spend half his time here; and Miss Darcy is always down for the summer months." Except, thought Elizabeth, "when she goes to Ramsgate."'

In *Mansfield Park*, when telling a story of a visit to Ramsgate, Tom Bertram gives a description of the kind of impropriety tolerated in watering places. He forms a new acquaintance on the pier, an inappropriate beginning in itself. Mrs Sneyd is 'surrounded by men' and the two Miss Sneyds are left to the company of other strange young men. Moreover, it transpires that the youngest Miss Sneyd, though 'perfectly easy in her manners, and as ready to talk as to listen' and not demurely attired, is not even 'out' in society.

In Jane's time assemblies were held in the Albion Hotel seen on the left in this contemporary print. (Courtesy of Terry Wheeler, Ramsgate Historical Society)

The Albion Hotel was replaced by a bank and is now a branch of Pizza Express.

Banker Nathaniel Austen, a very distant cousin of Jane's family, lived in this house further up the High Street on the left hand side. As a prominent member of Ramsgate society, Nathaniel would most likely have been known to Francis and possibly to Jane.

19. Deal

In Jane Austen's time Deal was famous (or infamous) for three things. It was a garrison town, it had a unique anchorage for merchant ships of the East India Company in an off-shore area of sandbanks known as 'the Downs' and it was England's most notorious centre for smuggling.

Duties were imposed on a huge range of items to fund the succession of foreign wars. Between 1700 and 1850 a quarter of the country's import/export trade was illegal and Deal boatmen were in the forefront of the activity. Much of the tea that Jane enjoyed during her lifetime would have been smuggled through Deal.

Middle Street, in the conservation heart of Deal, runs parallel to the sea front between Beach Street and High Street. In 1813 Jane said of her brother Frank and his wife Mary: 'I think they must soon have lodged in every house in the Town.'

St George the Martyr in Deal where Lord Nelson and Frank Austen regularly worshipped.

The box pews on the ground floor of the magnificent St George's church have been removed but many splendid features remain, including the gallery.

Jane mentions the town frequently in her letters but it appears only once in a novel. In *Persuasion*, Jane informs her readers that Deal is the only place where Admiral Croft's wife Sophy was ever ill, as it was the only place she was ever separated from him, whilst he was patrolling the North Sea.

The first mention of Deal in Jane's letters is when she was twenty-four and living at home in Steventon. She writes about Charles, the youngest of her two sailor brothers, who was twenty at the time and about to join a ship at Deal:

'Charles leaves us to-night. The "Tamar" is in the Downs, and Mr. Daysh advises him to join her there directly, as there is no chance of her going to the westward. Charles does not approve of this at all, and will not be much grieved if he should be too late for her before she sails, as he may then hope to get into a better station. He attempted to go to town last night, and got as far on his road thither as Dean Gate; but both the coaches were full, and we had the pleasure of seeing him back again. He will call on Daysh to-morrow to know whether the "Tamar" has sailed or not, and if she is still at the Downs he will proceed in one of the night coaches to Deal.'

On the evening of 29 July 1801 Lord Nelson arrived in Deal to take up his position of

second-in-command of the Channel Fleet. He was staying at the Royal Hotel and wrote to his friends Sir William and Lady Hamilton urging them to come to Deal: 'I hate the Downs but if my friends come it will be paradise.' On 12 October 1813 Jane commented: 'Southey's Life of Nelson – I am tired of Lives of Nelson, being that I never read any. I will read this however if Frank is mentioned in it.' Nelson himself wrote very favourably of Frank but Southey makes no mention of him in his book.

In 1805, when Jane is staying at Goodnestone, certain ladies of East Kent, Harriet (Jane spells it Harriot) Bridges in particular, were becoming very agitated about the plans for a ball to be held at the Garrison in Deal. It was to be a ticket only affair and, on the male side, open only to officers, which meant the men of the Bridges family were not invited. Writing from Goodnestone on 27 August Jane tells Cassandra:

'We had a very pleasant drive from Canterbury, and reached this place [Goodnestone Farm] about half-past four, which seemed to bid fair for a punctual dinner at five; but scenes of great agitation awaited us, and there was much to be endured and done before we could sit down to table.

'Harriot found a letter from Louisa Hatton, desiring to know if she and her brothers were to be at the ball at Deal on Friday, and saying that the Eastwell family had some idea of going to it, and were to make use of Rowling if they did; and while I was dressing she came to me with another letter in her hand, in great perplexity. It was from Captain Woodford, containing a message from Lady Forbes, which he had intended to deliver in person, but had been prevented from doing.

'The offer of a ticket for this grand ball, with an invitation to come to her house at Dover before and after it, was Lady Forbes' message. Harriot was at first very little inclined, or rather totally disinclined, to profit by her ladyship's attention; but at length, after many debates, she was persuaded by me and herself together to accept the ticket. The offer of dressing and sleeping at Dover she determined on Marianne's account to decline, and her plan is to be conveyed by Lady Elizabeth Hatton.'

It transpired that all the consternation about the ball was to no avail. The event was cancelled due to the death of the Duke of Gloucester, brother of King George III, who died in his sixty-second year.

As we have seen, Frank left Ramsgate when he received a commission for the *Leopard*, a 50 gun ship-of-the-line. From 1807 to 1809 he commanded the *St Albans* and made at least two voyages convoying home merchant ships of the East India Company. During the first week of July 1808 Jane's brother Henry paid one of his flying visits from London to join the house party at Godmersham. He and brother James went to Deal to welcome Frank, who had just arrived there in the *St Albans*.

From July 1811 Frank had been commanding the 74 gun *Elephant* as part of Admiral Young's North Sea Fleet, mostly engaged in blockading Napoleon's great dockyard at Flushing. Frank's wife Mary had moved from Ramsgate to Deal in order to be near him

Contraband Cottage in Middle Street gives a clue to the livelihoods of previous residents. Opposite is number 73 where Admiral Nelson's friend Captain Parker lived and died.

The Royal Hotel stands on the beach and in his invitation to the Hamiltons Lord Nelson said he hoped they: 'would not be disturbed by the sound of the surf'.

whenever he was in port causing Jane to write on 16 February 1813: 'I have a Letter from Frank; they are all at Deal again, established once more in fresh Lodgings. I think they must soon have lodged in every house in the Town. We read of the *Pyramus* being returned into Port, with interest – & fear Mrs D. D. will be regretting that she came away so soon. – There is no being up to the tricks of the Sea.' Mrs D. D. was the wife of Captain Deans Dundas. The captain and his wife were friends of Mary Lloyd. Frank's fourth child, George was born in Deal on 20 October 1812.

When they were ashore in Deal, Frank and Lord Nelson regularly worshipped at St George the Martyr church. Francis Austen was a strict disciplinarian aboard ship, as was his duty, but also a very religious man. His nephew James-Edward Austen reported that: 'He was spoken of as "the officer who kneeled at church."'

20. Sandling, Saltwood and Hythe

SANDLING

As we have seen in the chapter on Goodnestone, the Holy Cross church on the estate was in 1794 the scene of a joint wedding ceremony when Elizabeth Bridges married Jane's brother Edward and Elizabeth's sister Sophia married William Deedes of Sandling.

A year earlier, in an exchange of property, William Deedes had acquired Sandling Park from Sir Brook Bridges. The swap also included the neighbouring estate of Saltwood with its historic castle. William set about remodelling the old mansion at Sandling and employed the Italian architect Bonomi.

Elizabeth and Edward lived first at Rowling and later at Godmersham, both within an easy journey of Sandling. As siblings Elizabeth and Sophia were close and there were regular visits between the families in all three houses.

During Jane's visits to East Kent she was swept up in this social activity and her letters frequently mention family gatherings. We know that she visited Sandling at least twice. Her first mention of it is in a letter of 25 October 1800: 'In talking of Mr. Deedes' new house, Mrs. Bramston told us one circumstance, which, that we should be ignorant of it before, must make Edward's conscience fly into his face; she told us that one of the sitting rooms at Sandling, an oval room, with a bow at one end, has the very remarkable and singular feature of a fireplace with a window, the centre window of the bow, exactly over the mantel-piece.'

Jane returned to Godmersham early in September 1805 while Edward and Elizabeth took Fanny to London shopping, sightseeing and theatre going. During this time Jane and Cassandra stayed with Sophia at Sandling. Writing from Godmersham three years later on 15 June 1808, Jane says: 'I was agreeably surprised to find Louisa Bridges still here. She looks remarkably well (legacies are very wholesome diet), and is just what she always was. John [Bridges] is at Sandling. You may fancy our dinner party therefore; Fanny, of course, belonging to it, and little Edward, for that day.'

In the summer Jane wrote about her brother James visiting Sandling: 'James and Edward are gone to Sandling to-day – a nice scheme for James, as it will show him a new and fine country. Edward certainly excels in doing the honours to his visitors, and providing for their amusement. They come back this evening.'

In 1813 Jane made her last visit to East Kent and in a letter of 26 October, she left us

This new house, built in Georgian style, stands on the site of the mansion that Jane knew. The Bonomi-designed house was sadly destroyed by enemy action in 1942.

The gardens at Sandling, which were the pride of the Hardy family, are open for charity one day a year under the National Gardens Scheme.

with her impression of William Deedes: 'Mr. Deedes and Sir Brook – I do not care for Sir Brook's being a baronet; I will put Mr. Deedes first because I like him a great deal the best. They arrived together yesterday, for the Bridges are staying at Sandling, just before dinner; both gentlemen much as they used to be, only growing a little older. They leave us to-morrow.'

In 1897 Sandling was sold to the Rt Hon. Lawrence Hardy MP, who in that year invited the landscape designer Henry Milner to prepare a plan for the gardens. The estate passed to Hardy's son, Major A. E. Hardy and then to his grandson, Captain A. Hardy, the Hardy family being responsible for most of the present ornamental woodland gardens.

The mansion was sadly destroyed by enemy action in 1942, and the late Major Hardy built the present house on the site. Today Sandling estate is held in trust for the Hardy family and is not open to the public. However, the gardens are open for charity one day a year under the National Gardens Scheme.

SALTWOOD

At fifteen, Jane Austen wrote her humorous *History of England, by a partial, prejudiced, & ignorant Historian* which included illustrations by Cassandra. Jane mockingly imitates the style of textbook histories of English monarchs while ridiculing historians' pretensions to objectivity.

The period of history Jane chose to describe was: 'from the reign of Henry the 4th to the death of Charles the 1st' but she would have been very aware of Henry II's part in the death of Thomas Becket and the role Saltwood Castle played. The steadily deteriorating relations the king had with his archbishop culminated in his famous outburst on Christmas Day 1170:

Two pages of Jane Austen's History of England *with illustrations by Cassandra.*

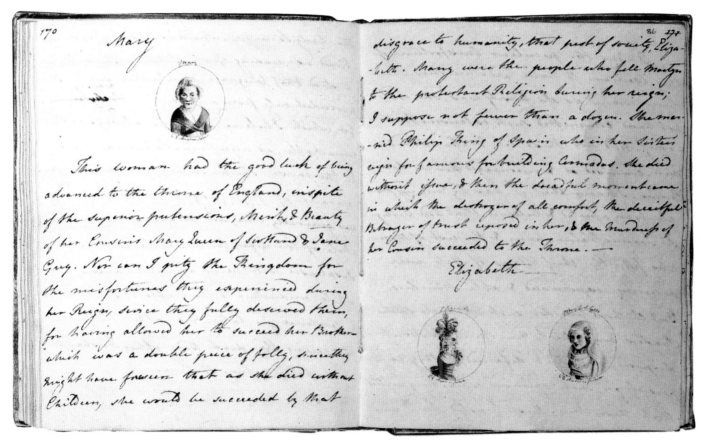

In Jane's time Saltwood Castle was acquired by William Deedes in a land swap deal with his father-in-law Sir Brook Bridges of Goodnestone.

'What sluggard wretches, what cowards have I brought up in my court, who care nothing for their allegiance to their Master! Not one will deliver me from this turbulent Priest!'

The four knights who accepted this challenge travelled from Normandy and stopped overnight at Saltwood to confer with Sir Ranulf de Broc, one of Henry's fiercest barons. De Broc gave them details of how they might perpetrate their villainy and provided an escort of his cavalry for their journey along Stone Street to Canterbury.

For centuries, until the reign of Henry VIII, Saltwood Castle had served as palace for a succession of Archbishops of Canterbury. In 1540 Archbishop Cranmer: '...observing the murmurs and envy that his possessions of this and sumptuous houses brought on him found himself obliged to part with it and conveyed it back to the crown.'

Although Jane skips the first seven Henrys she does make reference to King Henry VIII's abolition of religious houses when she says: 'The Crimes & Cruelties of this Prince, were too numerous to be mentioned, (as this history I trust has fully shewn) & nothing can be said in his vindication, but that his abolishing Religious Houses & leaving them to the ruinous depredations of time has been of infinite use to the landscape of England in general'. However, it was not Henry who was responsible for 'the ruinous depredations' at Saltwood, it was the great earthquake that occurred forty years later.

When she lived in Southampton Jane was keen to see the desecrated Netley Abbey. Saltwood is only a short distance from Sandling and it seems very likely she would have visited the castle which, in her time, was a romantic ruin. There is a note in Fanny Knight's

*Part of the inner bailey at
Saltwood Castle.*

*The lower entrance hall at
Saltwood Castle.*

*The gardens at Saltwood are
open on certain days in the year
to help raise funds for the
continued restoration of the
castle.*

125

diary about Jane's brother Henry, when staying at Godmersham, driving his wife Eliza over to see Saltwood Castle.

Margaret, Lady FitzWalter, of Goodnestone was born at Saltwood. Her brother Bill Deedes, the former Conservative politician and editor of the *Daily Telegraph*, has written of his childhood spent at the castle. In 1955 it was purchased by the art historian Lord Clark and later inherited by his son Alan Clark who was a minister in Margaret Thatcher's government. Today the castle is privately owned by Alan's widow, Jane Clark, and the gardens are open on certain days in the year to help raise funds for the continued restoration.

HYTHE

From 1803 during her visits to South East Kent, Jane would have been aware of the massive precautions taking place along the coastline to combat an impending invasion from Napoleon's Grande Armée. Prime Minister William Pitt the younger, supported by King George III, planned the 'Royal' Military Canal which was built between 1804 and 1809.

This strategic defensive measure, which today is designated an 'Ancient Monument', was known as 'Pitt's Ditch'. It is 9 feet deep by 30 feet wide and runs for 28 miles from Seabrook in Kent, through Hythe, to Cliff End near Hastings in East Sussex. It is the third

This early print of Hythe church with the row of Martello towers in the background is a scene which would have been familiar to Jane.

The Royal Military Canal at Hythe.

On the bank there are statues of the soldiers who defended the canal and the men who dug it.

longest defensive monument in the British Isles after Hadrian's Wall and Offa's Dyke. Hitler had to take account of this formidable obstacle in planning his invasion of Britain. In 'Operation Sea Lion' he assigned 7 Paratroop Division of 16 Army Group to take the canal bridges.

Between 1804 and 1812 the authorities also built a chain of small forts known as Martello towers to defend the south and east coast of England. Forty-seven of the towers have survived a few of which have been restored and transformed into museums. The towers are about 40 feet high with walls about 8 feet thick. The ground floor served as the magazine and storerooms for ammunition, equipment, water and provisions. Each was garrisoned by 24 men and one officer who lived on the first floor, which was divided into several rooms with fireplaces built into the walls for cooking and heating. The accommodation was divided into two separate rooms of almost equal size. The officer had one and the soldiers shared the other.

21. Wrotham

Edward Austen's wife, Elizabeth Bridges had a sister Harriet (Jane spells it Harriot) who married the Rev'd George Moore, eldest son of the Archbishop of Canterbury. Moore was rector of the beautiful village of Wrotham which lies among the western Kentish hills 2 miles east of St Clere. It was said to be the best living in Kent and as such, usually reserved for close relatives of the archbishop.

On 26 October 1813 Jane was staying at Godmersham and looking forward to visiting Wrotham on her way to her brother Henry's London house in Henrietta Street. In a letter to Cassandra she says:

Court Lodge, the Grade II listed rectory at Wrotham visited by Jane in November 1813.

The view of Wrotham church tower from the principal bedroom of Court Lodge.

The interior of St George's church, Wrotham where Jane worshipped twice on Sunday 14 November 1813

The memorial to the hated Rev'd Moore in St George's church declares he had 'unvarying kindness and affection' for his children.

'It seems now quite settled, that we go to Wrotham on Saturday, the 13th [November] spend Sunday there and proceed to London on Monday. I like the plan. I shall be glad to see Wrotham.'

Rev'd George Moore had demolished the rectory when he arrived in the parish and had commissioned the respected architect Samuel Wyatt to build a replacement in 1801/2. Its classical front and domed bay windows were almost as impressive a sight as the ruins of the former episcopal palace nearby.

On Saturday 13 November 1813 Jane travelled from Godmersham accompanied by brother Edward and his daughter Fanny. In her diary Fanny records 'baiting some time at Lenham' and attending the fine old church in the heart of Wrotham village twice on the Sunday.

In the letter of 26 October Jane reported an amusing incident she witnessed when Rev'd Moore was visiting Godmersham:

'Owing to a difference of clocks the coachman did not bring the carriage so soon as he ought by half an hour; anything like a breach of punctuality was a great offence, and Mr. Moore was very angry, which I was rather glad of. I wanted to see him angry; and, though he spoke to his servant in a very loud voice and with a good deal of heat, I was happy to perceive that he did not scold Harriot at all. Indeed, there is nothing to object to in his manners to her, and I do believe that he makes her – or she makes herself – very happy. They do not spoil their boy.'

The fact that Jane said 'I wanted to see him angry' suggests she was aware of his reputation. In 1806, some years after completing his *Topographical Survey of the County of Kent*, the historian Edward Hasted noted under Wrotham that:

'The Rector Mr Moore is so universally hated here that when he made his first appearance in Church, on his marriage to Miss Bridges, to shew it the clerk put up & they sung the funeral hymn instead of the usual Nupital Psalm.'

The Grade II listed rectory has been completely restored and survives today as Court Lodge, the ten bedroom show-piece property in an otherwise modern development of executive homes built with Georgian classical proportions.

An artist's impression of Court Lodge as it will look when the restoration is complete.

East Kent Memories

Writing of Kent in his book *The World of Jane Austen*, Nigel Nicolson observed: 'A glance at a contemporary map shows gentlemen's estates, large and small, overlapping each other like water-lily leaves on a pond.'

This remained the case through Victorian times and comic versifier R. H. Barham provides us with a list of guests at an East Kent society wedding. With the exception of Norton and Fairfax all these families appear regularly in Jane's letters:

It would bore you to death should I pause to describe,
Or enumerate half of the elegant tribe
Who fill'd the back-ground,
And among whom were found
The elite of the old county families round,
Such as Honeywood, Oxenden, Knatchbull, and Norton,
Matthew Robinson, too, with his beard, from Monk's Horton,
The Faggs, and Finch-Hattons, Tokes, Derings, and Deedses,
And Fairfax, (who then called the Castle of Leeds his).

The estates of East Kent and the great houses that Jane knew, or knew of, have experienced mixed fortunes during the succeeding two hundred years. Godmersham is now a college for opticians and Goodnestone, which has seen difficult days, is now poised for a new lease of life, to be funded in part by offering holiday apartments. The beautiful manor house of Rowling on the Goodnestone estate remains in private hands as does its dower house and the properties of Provender and the dower house of Norton Court near Ospringe.

Mersham le Hatch and Chilham Castle continue to function as family homes under private ownership. Godinton is maintained as near original by a private trust. Broome Park at Barham is now part of a country club and is divided into time-share apartments. The mansion of Mystole has been developed as luxury apartments and the present Eastwell Manor is now a quality country hotel.

Our introduction to these places and the people who lived in them in the eighteenth and early nineteenth centuries has been through the courtesy of a young woman who lived on the periphery of this world but was able to enter it through her family connections. In her letters and novels Jane Austen paints pen portraits for us to wonder at and contemplate.

Part of the physical world she knew and reported on has disappeared. The mansions at Patrixbourne, Elmsted, Nackington and Nonnington are no more but there are still clues to their locations and the impact they once had on their local neighbourhood.

NACKINGTON

Nackington House was one of the first in East Kent which Jane visited, dining there and returning to Rowling by moonlight, and was the home of Richard Milles MP for Canterbury. Jane wrote to Cassandra:

'We went in our two carriages to Nackington; but how we divided I shall leave you to surmise, merely observing that as Elizabeth and I were without either hat or bonnet, it would not have been very convenient for us to go in the chaise… Mrs Milles, Mr John Toke, and in short everybody of any Sensibility enquired in tender Strains after You.'

Only the stable block at Nackington remains with the buildings converted into comfortable family homes.

Above: *Nackington House was one of the first houses in East Kent which Jane visited.*

Left: *Only the stable block at Nackington remains and the buildings have been converted into comfortable family homes.*

Below: *Mrs Lewis Thomas Watson (née Mary Elizabeth Milles) of Nackington Court.*

Opposite: *'We went by Bifrons, and I contemplated with a melancholy pleasure the abode of him on whom I once fondly doated.'*

BIFRONS

'We went by Bifrons, and I contemplated with a melancholy pleasure the abode of him on whom I once fondly doated.' Jane is writing here about the home of Edward Taylor, who had 'such beautiful dark eyes' and of whom Jane and Cassandra both became enamoured.

In 1800, Taylor was a captain in the Romney Fencible Dragoons and in 1802 he married Louisa Beckington, daughter of Rev. J. C. Beckington of Bourne in Kent. In 1807 Taylor was elected Member of Parliament for Canterbury, a seat he held until 1812.

The Conyngham family, the last owners of Bifrons, moved away in 1874 and the house was let until 1939 when it was requisitioned by the Army. By 1945 it was judged too damaged to be worth repair and was demolished, leaving only a stable block, some fine trees in the park and an elegant bridge over the River Nailbourne.

The two lodge houses at Bifrons remain today as private homes.

134

Top left: *This attractive Georgian bridge on the estate, has recently been restored and carries a bridleway over the River Nailbourne.*

Top right: *The pathway which once led from St Mary's church to Bifrons is now overgrown and impassable.*

Right: *This double line of fine trees once flanked the carriage drive up to the great house of Bifrons.*

EVINGTON

In Jane Austen's day Evington at Elmsted was the home of the Honeywood baronet family. In a letter of 6 November 1813 we hear of Lady Honeywood visiting Godmersham on her way home from Eastwell and of Jane's approval of her:

'I have extended my lights and increased my acquaintance a good deal within these two days. Lady Honywood you know; I did not sit near enough to be a perfect judge, but I thought her extremely pretty, and her manners have all the recommendations of ease and good humour and unaffectedness; and, going about with four horses and nicely dressed herself, she is altogether a perfect sort of woman.'

Evington stood empty during the First World War and was demolished in 1938.

Elmsted church where the Honeywoods worshipped has a unique tower built of flint with an overhanging storey of shingle, crowned with a small steeple.

Top: *Among the tombs of the Honeywoods is that of Sir John, who died in 1781. It bears the following inscription: 'We read in times when hospitality and simplicity of manners were giving way to fashion, Sir John maintained them pure and incorrupt.'*

This circle of trees marks the spot where Evington manor stood in Jane Austen's time.

A cluster of red brick outbuildings are all that remain to be seen at Fredville.

Opposite: *The coach road which runs past the old gatekeeper's lodge at Fredville is now a public foot-path (with no vehicular right of way).*

138

FREDVILLE

On 18 November, 1814, Jane wrote to Fanny Knight offering guidance about her feelings for her admirers commenting on Fanny's infatuation and love towards a certain 'Mr. A' who apparently managed to steal Fanny's heart: 'Your mistake has been one that thousands of women fall into. He was the first young man who attached himself to you. That was the charm and most powerful it is.' 'Mr A' was Lord Brabourne's invention to disguise the genuine name of Mr Plumptre when he published Jane's letters in the 1880s.

Later on, Jane is adamant that Fanny must give up John Pemberton Plumptre, of Fredville near Nonnington: 'Anything is to be preferred or endured rather than marrying

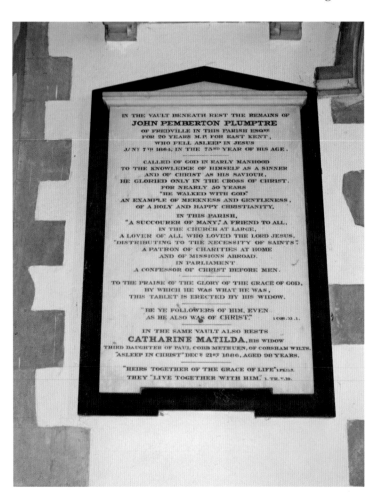

without affection; and, if his deficiencies of manner strike you more than all his good qualities, if you continue to think strongly of them, give him up at once.'

John Pemberton Plumptre married Catherine Methuen in 1818 and in 1820 Fanny married Sir Edward Knatchbull, a widower some years older than herself, and went on to have nine children.

Fredville House was a school in the 1920s and 1930s then commandeered by the Army in the Second World War and suffered fire damage. The remainder of the building was demolished post war. The park is publicly accessible and since the late eighteenth century has been renowned for its magnificent trees, especially its oaks and chestnuts.

William Hasted wrote in his *History and Topographical Survey of the County of Kent* in the late 1790s: 'At a small distance from the front of Fredville-house, stands the remarkable large oak tree, usually known by the name of the Fredville oak. It measures twenty-seven feet round in the girth, and is about thirty feet in height; and though it must have existed for many centuries, yet it looks healthy and thriving, and has a most majestic and venerable appearance.'

Epilogue

Anne Sharp with whom Jane found a truly compatible spirit and formed a lasting relationship.

Between 1794 and 1813 Jane Austen made at least nine extended visits to East Kent but, outside of her family, she seems to have kept in touch with only one person of all those mentioned in her letters. That person was Anne Sharp, Fanny Knight's governess at Godmersham from 1804 to 1806.

In July 1806 some of the Bridges' in-laws joined the house party at Godmersham and three years afterwards Jane remembered how 'animated' she and Cassandra had been when talking with Harriet Bridges and Anne Sharp.

Anne resigned her post at Godmersham due to ill health which begs a few questions as she held a number of subsequent positions as governess and lady's companion and by 1823 she was running her own boarding-school for girls in Liverpool.

A year older than Jane, Anne was in a similar precarious financial position. Governesses were often considered merely superior servants and Jane's warm regard and friendship for Anne shows a commendable lack of snobbery. In 1809 Jane wrote to Cassandra that 'Miss Sharp… is born, poor thing! to struggle with Evil…'

It is clear that some members of the wealthy county set of East Kent regarded Jane as the poor relation. On occasion she encountered the worst aspects of English class snobbery from affluent people who believed that wealth was either the cause or result of superiority, or both. I believe she may have used this experience to create some of her most memorable characters like Sir Walter Elliot and Lady Catherine de Bourgh.

It is interesting that Jane's nephew, James Edward Austen-Leigh had a different perspective on Anne Sharp; he described her as: 'horridly affected but rather amusing'.

Although Jane was modest, it is clear she was intellectually superior to the majority of people she met throughout her life. This may account partly for her failing to find a husband. In Anne Sharp she found a truly compatible spirit with whom she formed a lasting relationship. Claire Tomalin in *Jane Austen a Life*, summarised this when she said: 'Anne occupied the unique position in Jane's life as the necessary, intelligent friend.'

Jane also valued Anne's opinion of her writing. On 3 November 1813 Jane wrote to Cassandra: '…I have more of such sweet flattery from Miss Sharp! – She is an excellent kind friend' (which may refer to Anne Sharp's opinion of *Pride and Prejudice*). It is known that Anne Sharp thought *Mansfield Park* 'excellent' but she preferred *Pride and Prejudice* and rated *Emma* 'between the two'.

In May 1817 it was clear Jane Austen's health was failing. She was probably suffering from Addison's disease, curable now but lethal then. She had taken lodgings in a house in Winchester to be near the doctor who was treating her. On 18 July 1817, at about 4.30 in the morning Jane died in the arms of her sister Cassandra. There is one known extant letter from Jane to Anne Sharp, dated 22 May 1817. It is addressed to 'my dearest Anne' and begins:

'Your kind Letter my dearest Anne found me in bed, for in spite of my hopes & promises when I wrote to you I have since been very ill indeed. An attack of my sad complaint seized me within a few days afterwards – the most severe I ever had – & coming upon me after weeks of indisposition, it reduced me very low. I have kept my bed since 13. of April, with only removals to a Sopha. Now, I am getting well again, & indeed have been gradually tho' slowly recovering my strength for the last three weeks.'

The letter continues with a description of Jane's situation and concludes: 'If I live to be an old Woman I must expect to wish I had died now, blessed in the tenderness of such a Family, & before I had survived either them or their affection, – You would have held the memory of your friend Jane too in tender regret I am sure. – But the Providence of God has restored me – & may I be more fit to appear before him when I am summoned, than I sh'd have been now! – Sick or Well, believe me ever your attached friend. J. Austen.'

Anne Sharp is known to have visited Chawton on at least two occasions: in June 1815 and in August/September 1820. After Jane's death, Cassandra wrote to Anne on 28 July 1817 sending a 'lock of hair you wish for, and I add a pair of clasps which she sometimes wore and a small bodkin which she had had in constant use for more than twenty years.'

Emma was the fourth and final novel to be published in Jane's lifetime. As author, she had been allocated twelve of the three volume presentation copies by the publisher John Murray. Of these, nine were sent to family members (including Jane herself), one to the librarian of the Prince Regent (to whom the work was dedicated), and one to Countess Morley, these last two sets under obligation from the publisher.

Jane made a gift of the remaining three volume set to Anne. This was the only set given to a personal friend, testament to the strength of Jane's feelings for Anne Sharp.

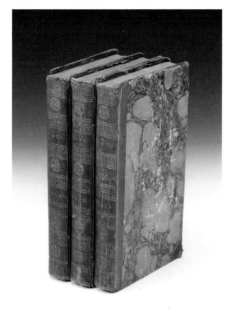

The three volume presentation set of Emma *gifted to Anne Sharp by Jane.*

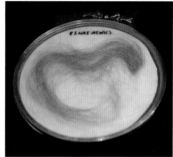

The lock of Jane's hair now preserved at Chawton House Museum which Cassandra sent to Anne Sharp.

Bibliography

A Chronology of Jane Austen and Her Family	Deirdre Le Faye
A Memoir of Jane Austen	J.E. Austen-Leigh
Jane Austen – A Family Record	Deirdre Le Faye
Jane Austen – A life	Claire Tomalin
Jane Austen in Kent	David Waldron Smithers
Jane Austen's Letters – Collected and Edited	Deirdre Le Faye
Jane Austen's World	Maggie Lane
Sanditon	Jane Austen
The History of England	Jane Austen
The World of Jane Austen	Nigel Nicolson